I0820416

IMAGES
of America
LGBTQ WICHITA

On the Cover: A Pride rally in the 1990s features a section of the rainbow flag, a flag that was itself a creation of Kansan Gilbert Baker. (Courtesy of Jennifer King.)

The Center of Wichita

ISBN 978-1-4671-6249-4

Published by Arcadia Publishing
Charleston, South Carolina

Printed in the United States of America

Library of Congress Control Number: 2025932009

For all general information, please contact Arcadia Publishing:
Telephone 843-853-2070
Fax 843-853-0044
E-mail sales@arcadiapublishing.com

Visit us on the Internet at www.arcadiapublishing.com

For those who stood up when it was difficult
for those who could not

Contents

Acknowledgments

This project has involved people who have served in many capacities. Thanks, Christen Brouillette and Amanda Mathews, for helping get us started. The writing team included Darbee Chard, Brent Kennedy, Derek Landwehr, and Jay M. Price and is grateful to all the people and groups who have made this possible by sharing their collections and memories. These include the Center of Wichita, GLSEN, Positive Directions, College Hill United Methodist, Pine Valley Christian Church, First Metropolitan Community Church/Table of Hope Metropolitan Community Church, the *Gayly*, the Heart of America Men's Chorus, KAKE-TV, J's Lounge, the *Liberty Press*, the National Park Service, Our Fantasy, Planet Hair, Sedgwick County Records Management, the Sisters of the Precious Blood, the Sisters of Perpetual Indulgence, St. James Episcopal Church, the *Sunflower*, the Wichita Prime Timers, Rain, XY, Unity of Wichita, the University of Kansas School of Medicine, *The Wichita Eagle*, Wichita State University's Belonging Plaza, and Wichita State University's Spectrum: LGBTQ & Allies. Thanks to Phil Cunningham and the Under the Rainbow Oral History Project at University of Kansas (KU); the Bruce McKinney Archives at the University of Kansas and Stuart Hines at Special Collections & Archives, University Libraries, Missouri Valley Special Collections, University of Missouri–Kansas City (UMKC); the Gay and Lesbian Archive of Mid-America at the University of Missouri, Kansas City; the Wichita-Sedgwick County Historical Museum; Mary Nelson and Wichita State University's Department of Special Collections; Wichita State University Libraries, Special Collections and University Archives; Michelle Enke and the Wichita Public Library; the Kansas Historical Society (KSHS); and Women Without Purses. Thanks also to all the individuals who contributed to the project, including Ron Anderson, Eileen Ball, David Barker, Jay Basham, Michael Bayouth, Gregory Boyd, Robert Branaman, Benjamin and Curtis Breese-Isley, Kevin Brown, Richard Brown, Gary Butterfield, Rev. Jackie Carter, Samantha Carter, Nolin Christensen, Connie Clark, Deb Davis, Robin Dormer, Dead Orchestra, Jason Dilts, Donna DiTriani, Tracy Fahrbach, Mother Dawn Frankfurt, Deb Davis, Jim Fenton, Gary Gardenhire, Jon Ginoli, Michelle Guoladdle, Rev. David Hansen, Dawn Harris, Randy Harrison, Michael Kasselman, Lyle Kee, Jennifer King, George Laughead, Valda Lewis, Medford Logsdon, Dan Manning, Hugo Marquez, Robby Martinez, Jim Martinson, Martin Mendoza, Paula Moore, Virginia Scott Norton, Cody Patton, Jennifer Pearson, Chris Pumpelly, Brad Purkey, Dave Quick, Sgt. Vanessa Rusco, Brianna Southworth, Phil Speary, Staci Steddum, Dr. Donna Sweet, Dudley Dodgion Toevs, Tyler Thornton, Jami Tracy, Sister Theresa Wetta, Brandon Whipple, Kerry Wilks, Tim Wood, and James Woods.

Many of the people who are discussed here may have been "out, loud, and proud," but their photographs and mementos remain in the closet—or the attic—or the basement—or the back shed. The hope is that this book encourages more individuals to preserve and share their photographs and memories. If not credited, photographs are courtesy of the Center of Wichita.

INTRODUCTION

How do you document what wants to be invisible?

—Phil Speary

LGBTQ persons have been part of Wichita's history from the beginning. They include residents of the city but also those who lived in the surrounding small towns and farms who found in Wichita a place to be themselves and connect with others. Documenting this history, however, can be difficult in a place like Kansas until the mid-20th century. Until the 1960s, evidence came from criminal records or speculations from cryptic statements and inferences from personal reflections. Beyond the crime records and vice headlines, LGBTQ individuals lived lives hidden among the "confirmed bachelors," unmarried schoolmarms, the marriages of convenience, and the local gossips who insisted that "everyone knows that boy/girl from the farm down the road is a little odd."

There were subcultures where same-sex attraction and questioning of gender roles did take place. There were figures such as Berdache among tribal peoples. Groups of single individuals, from drovers along cattle drives to military outposts to the "tramps" and "hoboes" of the 1890s, all had reputations of being places where same-sex attraction took place. However, understanding these connections has been difficult given that the Victorian world did not connect emotional intimacy with sexuality the way our society does, and it was perfectly acceptable for a person to express passionate feelings to someone of the same gender regardless of their sexual orientation. It also provided cover in a time when survival depended on hiding out of sight.

Like all states into the twentieth century, Kansas law criminalized same-sex intimacy. The state's sodomy law predated statehood, created by the territorial "Bogus Legislature" in 1855, classified certain physical acts as a felony. These included acts between individuals of the same sex but, as upheld by cases such as *State v. Hulbert* in 1925, also extended to heterosexual couples, even married men and women. Heterosexual violations of the "crime against nature" remained illegal until 1969, but same-sex activity remained against the law. The US Supreme Court upheld sodomy laws in *Bowers v. Hardwick* in 1986. Attempts to get rid of Kansas's law have remained unsuccessful even after *Lawrence v. Texas* declared them unconstitutional. In a state that had prohibition from 1881 through 1949, homosexuality came to be associated with other vices akin to prostitution, illegal gambling, and drug use. Officials and the media decried homosexuals as deviants who skulked in the shadows. In the process, LGBTQ persons and establishments also found themselves in violation of laws against "lewd and lascivious behavior" or "solicitation and indecent acts."

With visibility dangerous and no public support whatsoever, forming long-term groups or associations was difficult at best, and what was there was an easy target for any law enforcement figure who wanted to show that he was "tough on crime." Even so, LGBTQ individuals existed in Wichita, often through informal networks of individuals. By World War II and afterward, the beginnings of a community began to emerge. It aligned with counterculture groups, especially in the 1960s. Several moved on to other areas like San Francisco and New York, with locals often quite content to think that homosexuality was something that happened elsewhere, not in a Great Plains city like Wichita.

The 1969 events at Stonewall in New York reverberated across the country, however. By the 1970s, changing attitudes included awareness and conversations in places like Wichita. As the decade unfolded, a community, with religious groups and advocacy bodies, started to bring what had been hidden in the shadows more into public view. In the span of a few years, people who had been in the shadows of the law were asking for recognition and even protection, culminating in Wichita's civil rights ordinance in 1977. The city's commission was clearly more open than the larger populace, who overturned the ordinance by public vote in 1978. The dashed hopes of the ordinance were followed a few years later by the HIV/AIDS crisis.

By the 1980s, however, LGBTQ Wichita was a different community from just a decade earlier. The AIDS crisis brought tragedy and struggle but also resources and networks. Clubs like Our Fantasy anchored a set of bars and clubs that had developed mostly on the city's south side. There were churches and groups within denominations. The development of Wichita Pride with a parade and a parallel set of political rallies brought public attention, both good and bad, to efforts. By now, the community was starting to see something that would have been unthinkable in earlier times: allies.

The 1990s saw what many have felt was the community's heyday. There were groups, businesses, and institutions that catered to a cautiously open clientele. The 1991 Pride parade was among the city's most visible but even then, people were scared to attend out of fear of violence or repercussions at work or among family. There were leading voices, such as those who appeared in the pages of the *Liberty Press*. There were drag contests, gay rodeos, and awards galas. There were subcultures that advocated for their expressions of LGBTQ identity and activity. AIDS activism brought with it its own efforts. Groups connected to youth and students worked to support LGBTQ folks. The national culture wrestled with gay characters on television and contradictory government politics. Protestors at events and denunciations from pulpits and conservative voices became rallying cries for activism and organized efforts.

The 21st century brought both hope and challenge. There were landmark Supreme Court rulings alongside the political battles in Topeka. There were calls to be part of the fabric of society: to be married, to adopt, to be ordained, to serve in the military, and to be elected. There were, at the same time, the deaths of the pioneers who had taken risks so that the next generations could pursue being part of that fabric.

Today, the community is in flux with issues of gender identity and trans issues, bringing a new layer to the discussion. The erosion of rights on the national and state levels unsettled those who fought so hard to get where they were. Through it all, however, one aspect is consistent: LGBTQ history is not just the story of New York and San Francisco. It is also the story of regional centers like Wichita. It is the story of the rural areas that Wichita supports. The community has been visible as such for over 55 years, but its members have roots that go much farther back.

A note here about what follows: being LGBTQ is a very private and personal matter and can be risky in a place like Kansas with few protections. Just because a person identified as gay or lesbian or went to clubs and events does not mean that they are comfortable with having their name and photograph used in a book. Therefore, this narrative skews toward groups, organizations, and activists who were comfortable being public about their sexuality. The countless ordinary lives that defined life in a place like Wichita will, sadly, get less coverage, not because they are not important, but because individuals were not always comfortable being so visible. The team debated this early on and has erred, when possible, on the side of not including persons out of respect for their privacy and safety. That said, the hope is that this book will inspire LGBTQ Wichitans to make efforts to preserve and document their lives. What survives is what we remember.

Jack Hufford, one of Wichita's best-known bar owners, and Sonny Walker pose for the camera about 1967. (Courtesy of Jennifer King.)

One

Friends of Dorothy

As long as it is just a rumor, it is safe. It's when things are confirmed that they get dangerous.

—Lyle Kee

People of diverse orientations and gender identities have been part of Kansas since before there was a Kansas. Wichita's early roots as a cowtown and boomtown offered a place to live a life different from the expectations of straight society. However, this was still challenging at best and often dangerous. Being hidden meant safety, so the city's earliest documented LGBTQ history was limited only to those who were unlucky enough or outspoken enough to make the papers. By the postwar years, however, enclaves and networks had started to quietly develop out of the public eye, setting the stage for more to come.

"Crimes against nature" were against the law, but so were activities that violated public sentiments of decency. By the middle of the 20th century, a newer model based on psychology saw homosexuality as a disorder to be treated rather than a crime to be punished. Even if not arrested, punished, or "treated," being found out could easily result in social ostracism, being fired, and being subject to harassment and violence without any recourse.

LGBTQ persons had to live in the shadows, fearful of being discovered. That said, larger cities like Wichita allowed a degree of anonymity not found in rural Kansas. By the 1950s and 1960s, a small network of LGBTQ persons and groups had formed, confirming that what happened in places like New York or San Francisco also took place on the Great Plains.

Discussing LGBTQ history before the middle of the 20th century is difficult, as the story of Owen B. Stocker illustrates. A respected entrepreneur in the construction and finishing business, Stocker never married and was known for attending "stag parties," like the one below. One party in Chicago had men perform a form of burlesque we might call "drag." He ended his days with a male roommate, and when asked about being single, he simply said, "My reasons for not marrying are private." However, based on surviving materials, there is no definitive way to know whether Stocker would have identified as gay, bisexual, asexual, or as a straight man who simply lived an eccentric life. (Both images courtesy of Wichita-Sedgwick County Historical Museum.)

Kansas Law 21-907 decreed certain physical acts were considered examples of the "detestable and abominable crime against nature." Whether done in homosexual or heterosexual contexts, convicted persons "shall be punished by confinement and hard labor not exceeding ten years." From 1930 to 1950, some 18 persons in Sedgwick County, all men, were charged with either a crime against nature or sodomy (excluding those whose charge involved children or other crimes such as assault). Early convictions were 10 years or more. By the 1940s, most charges were dismissed. By the 1950s, those charged with violating the "crimes against nature" law, presuming the charge did not entail violent acts or those against children, found themselves sentenced not to the penitentiary in Lansing but rather to the state mental facility in Larned, below. (Both images courtesy of the Kansas Historical Society, hereafter KSHS, and Kansas Memory.)

By the middle of the 20th century, the works of Sigmund Freud or, in Kansas, research at the Menninger Hospital in Topeka suggested homosexuality was a disorder rather than a crime. This perspective appears in a 1956 annual report that shows how crimes against nature were increasingly associated with mental illness. Meanwhile, works like the Kinsey Report suggested homosexual acts were far more common across the population. (Both images courtesy of KSHS.)

TABLE No. 5.—Criminal Insane—Admitted Since March 26, 1939—*Continued*

No.	Age	Legal residence	MENTAL DIAGNOSIS	Years confined	Crime committed
4720	26	Labette	Psychopathic personality without psychosis; pathological sexuality	4 mos.	Crime against nature
4272	43	Ellis	Dementia praecox, paranoid type	7	Assault
5006	56	Osage (Maine)	Dementia praecox, paranoid type	12	Forgery
5056	46	Osborne	Psychosis with syphilitic meningo encephalitis	10	Incest
5107	65	Doniphan	Psychopathic personality without psychosis	7	Arson
5196	55	Wyandotte	Dementia praecox, paranoid type	5	Murder
5279	35	Wyandotte	Prison psychosis	10	[illegible]
[illegible]	[illegible]	[illegible]			

In addition to specific acts, the Kansas code criminalized "open, gross lewdness, or lascivious behavior, or of any open and notorious act of public indecency." This meant that activities such as at parks or in bars could be subject to raids or entrapment by police. (Courtesy of Wichita State University Special Collections, hereafter WSU.)

The view that homosexuals were weak, disordered, and therefore "security risks" resulted in, for example, Kansas-raised Pres. Dwight Eisenhower signing Executive Order 10450 that banned homosexuals from working for the federal government. This document was the cornerstone of an expulsion of LGBTQ persons from federal employment known as "the Lavender Scare." (Courtesy of National Park Service.)

The outbreak of World War II transformed Wichita, which nearly doubled its population by the middle of the 1940s due to defense workers coming in from rural areas and other states to work in aviation like Boeing and other industries. Coming from rural parts of Kansas as well as the upper South, these arrivals included LGBTQ individuals who found limited freedom in the anonymity of urban life. (Courtesy of Jennifer King.)

After World War II, clubs emerged in cities across the region in places like Kansas City, Missouri, as seen here. Existing on the margins, these clubs and their patrons faced periodic raids on the part of the police. (Courtesy of the Gay and Lesbian Archive of Mid-America [GLAMA], University of Missouri–Kansas City.)

Author James Fugate, pictured right, from Holyrood, Kansas, under the pseudonym James Barr, wrote the book *Quatrefoil* in 1950. The story of the relationship between two servicemen in the 1940s. The book is one the first novels that featured a homosexual relationship as its main theme. In the 1950s, Barr returned to Kansas, where he wrote another collection of short stories about gay life in the oil fields, a collection called "Derricks." (Right, courtesy of WSU; below, courtesy authors' collection.)

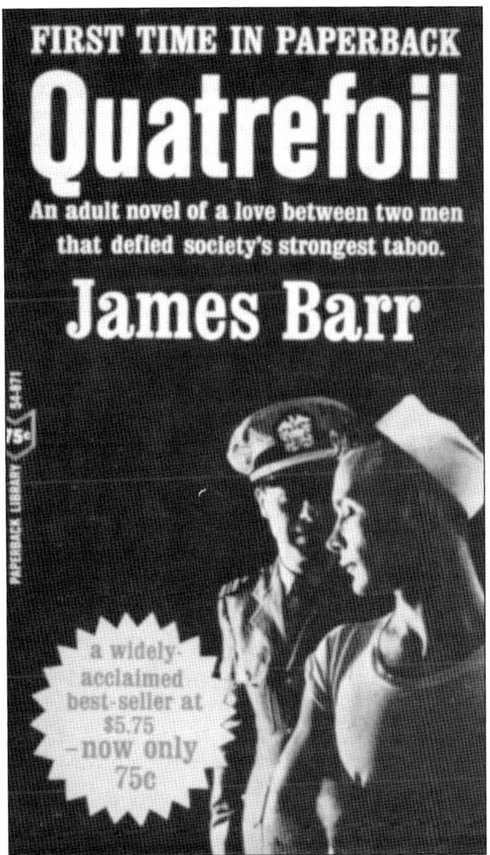

For "closeted" gay men, many contacts came from informal networks of anonymous meeting places across the city. One such "tea room" was this small Pueblo Deco–style building in Riverside Park, a site of cultural contention and change since its construction. The topic attracted a young Rev. Laud Humphreys, left, who was associate rector of St. James Episcopal Church and studying for a PhD in sociology. His 1968 dissertation, "Tearoom Trade: A Study of Homosexual Encounters in Public Places," became the subject of a groundbreaking 1971 book *Tearoom Trade: Impersonal Sex in Public Places*. The book was instrumental to the American Psychological Association (APA) removing homosexuality as a mental illness, but the work was also infamous for Humphreys's unethical methods, including following men back to their homes, potentially revealing their secrets to their families. (Above, courtesy of Brent Kennedy; left courtesy of St. James Episcopal Church.)

U. S. A.
Confidential
BY JACK LAIT
AND
LEE MORTIMER
CROWN PUBLISHERS, INC.
NEW YORK

"We offer as proof that America is being feminized the fact that tough and isolated Kansas is going homo," said Jack Lait and Lee Mortimer in their sensational *USA Confidential*. "Wichita cops are said to have a list of the names of 1,000 fairies who live in the city." The book continued that one "can find them mincing into the Blue Lantern or Curley's Roundhouse. The biggest fag parties are held in an apartment over a business building in the 1200 block of East Douglas [which would have been just beyond the Ben Robinson Buick photograph below]. You can go through three doors to an inner sanctum where an old fat fairy in a Japanese kimono makes like a geisha girl." (Right, courtesy of authors' collection; below, courtesy of WSU.)

Bars that served LGBTQ persons were a challenge in all states, but Kansas, with its convoluted liquor laws, made the situation even more complicated. For example, the 1965 Private Club Act allowed establishments to serve liquor by the drink but only in private clubs that offered memberships. One of the first of these clubs in Wichita was Jack's Jolly Jug, initially located on West Second Street. Below, Chalmers "Alice" Clark enjoys a drink there in 1967. (Both images courtesy of Connie Clark and Jennifer King.)

In 1970, Larry Schwein, Sonny Walker, and Jack Hufford, pictured from left to right, gather at the club called The Bus Station. (Courtesy of Jennifer King.)

Originally from Newton, Colleen "Coke" Didier came out in 1963. She appears here seated in front of a group of friends in the early 1970s. At the time, even being photographed like this was risky. "You didn't tell anybody that you were gay, especially where you worked," she recalled. (Courtesy of Jennifer King and Connie Clark.)

In the local counterculture scene, LGBTQ persons and the Beat movement often moved in the same circles. Wichita's Beat community included artists such as Bruce Conner, Michael McClure, Dave Haselwood, and Charles Plymell, seen left. Several Beat figures moved to San Francisco's West Coast Beat community. Charles Plymell played an important role in Allen Ginsburg's trip to Wichita in 1966. While in Wichita, Ginsberg gave a reading at Moody's Skid Row Beanery, later known as the Vortex/Magic Theatre and Club Bar and Watkins Sundries. Seen below, this site stood at the southeast corner of Douglas Avenue and St. Francis Street, now the site of Naftzger Park. (Both images courtesy of Wichita Public Library.)

In the 1960s, clubs that served the Beat movement and the counterculture also tended to be safe spaces for sexual minorities. One of these was the Chance's R on Douglas Avenue. When he visited the club on his trip to Wichita, Allen Ginsberg wrote a poem tribute that referred to "fairy boys of the plains and their gay sisters of the city step together to the center of the floor illumined by machine eyes, screaming drumbeat." In 1967, the *Evergreen Review Magazine* published this poster from local Beat artist Robert Branaman. The club has long since closed, but the building continued to serve countercultural clientele. (Courtesy of Robert Branaman.)

Allen Ginsberg, a gay man and poet of the Beat Generation, traveled the United States to perform his controversial political works. One tour passed through Wichita in early 1966 and moved to various cities in Kansas. A Wichita State University student-led effort sponsored Ginsberg and his lifelong partner, Peter Orlovsky, after faculty refusal. He presented the controversial "Wichita Vortex Sutra" on February 21, 1966. (Courtesy of WSU.)

While the beats represented a countercultural challenge to "straight" society, a number of "homophile" groups emerged across the country that advocated for civil rights for homosexual persons. A group called "One" from Kansas City was an example. On February 18, 1966, coincidentally, just as Allen Ginsburg was visiting Wichita, 40 individuals from across the country met in Kansas City to plan for a national organization. The movement became known as the North American Conference of Homophile Associations, or NACHO (pronounced "nay-ko"). (Courtesy of Missouri Valley Special Collections.)

Soon after the 1966 Kansas City NACHO meeting, individuals, including Drew Shafer, created an organization called Phoenix that became an important publishing center for the homophile movement. (Courtesy of GLAMA.)

Here, Ellie Elimon (center) and Linn Copeland (right) sit at a club in the late 1960s. Candid photographs like this are today one of the few ways community members were able to remember each other in an otherwise often hidden world. (Courtesy of Connie Clark and Jennifer King.)

Two

SHELTER IN PLACE

HOMOSEXUAL BILL OF RIGHTS

1. Private consensual sex between persons over the age of consent shall not be an offense.
2. Solicitation for any sexual acts shall not be an offense except upon the filing of a complaint by the aggrieved party, not a police officer or agent.
3. A person's sexual orientation or practice shall not be a factor in the granting or renewing of federal security clearances or visas, or in the granting of citizenship.
4. Service in and discharge from the Armed Forces and eligibility for veteran's benefits shall be without reference to homosexuality.
5. A person's sexual orientation or practice shall not affect his eligibility for employment with federal, state, or local governments, or private employers.

—adopted at the 1968 Chicago NACHO meeting

Starting in the 1960s, a new wave of activism and awareness emerged as individuals began to realize that they were not alone here in Kansas, but part of something larger. Clubs and social gatherings while also navigating both public attitudes and Kansas's liquor laws. Until 1987, Kansas only allowed the serving of alcohol in "private clubs," so every bar required patrons to have a "membership" to drink. There were clubs that could only sell beer, as one had to be over 21 to buy hard liquor. Being a "dance club" required its own license, and a bar without one could be shut down just because people decided to start dancing to the music.

Even so, organizations and groups developed to serve not just Wichita, but the region. Wichita seemed poised to be at the forefront of what was then called "the gay rights movement," with the passing of one of the nation's first ordinances. The following year, however, a popular referendum released the ordinance, affirming that the city's conservative reputation was still well-founded. A few years later, a community already on edge was devastated by the arrival of HIV/AIDS. The tragedy shattered lives and, at the same time, planted the seeds for groups and institutions that came to define LGBTQ life in Wichita.

News of the 1969 Stonewall Riot gave a young Martin Mendoza the courage to come out to his family. Already an activist in Chicano movements such as the United Farm Workers' grape boycott and the Brown Berets, Mendoza soon turned his focus to LGBTQ issues. Originally considering the priesthood, Mendoza found affirmation in the gay Catholic group Dignity and was a key leader in the founding of the Wichita chapter. The Sisters of the Precious Blood became a key source of support as chaplains, even though the bishop was outspoken against LGBTQ rights. (Courtesy of Martin Mendoza.)

Sue Campbell (left) and Connie Condray (right), seen here in the 1980s, were coworkers at the same company when they met in the 1970s and remained lifelong partners. Finding each other was more than good fortune; it was unusual given how risky it was to be gay or lesbian then. They recalled, "We were afraid to go to bars or even talk to each other at work." (Courtesy of Jennifer King.)

Raids and entrapment increased during election times, when politicians could campaign on being tough on law and order. Few were more visible than Sedgwick County sheriff and later Kansas attorney general Vern Miller, pictured here. Miller reveled in high-profile events against gay bars, in part against lewd behavior, but even more as part of his crusade against those who violated Kansas's absurdly complicated liquor laws. Courtesy of Sedgwick County Records Management. (Courtesy of Sedgwick County Records Management.)

The earliest Pride commemorations took place in bars because it was not safe to be out in public. The first named Pride Week took place in 1977 as a picnic at Sim Park shelter pictured here. It was the first daytime, outdoor 'public event' for the Lesbian/Gay community of Wichita. As Bruce McKinney remembered, "Fear of retaliation and violence was rampant. . . . The community and public kept driving through the park looking for [at] the picnic for nearly six hours."

THE NEW BUS STATION

H 69

EXP 2-24-85

Name Jim MARTINSON Date 2-24-84 # 21

Sign Jim Martinson OWNER Jan Jones MGR

In the 1960s, the city's bus station downtown was another semi-anonymous meeting place for LGBTQ persons. In the 1970s, a club opened on East Harry Street called the Bus Station, a humorous reference to those clandestine meetings. It then moved to 1117 E. Pawnee Street and merged with a local women's bar called Jekyll and Hyde's to be christened the New Bus Station. A longtime patron recalled fondly, "We ran our disco lights off of a car battery, those were the days!" (Courtesy of Jim Martinson.)

No 019 Expires 4-27-85

This certifies that

JIM MARTINSON

is a member in good standing and is entitled to the privileges thereof as governed by the laws of Kansas.

Paragon

A Class B Private Club

2835 George Washington Blvd.

Wichita, Kansas 67210

Authorized Signature

With the state's private club laws, bars had to issue "memberships" with cards, visibly identifying patrons. Additionally, those 18 and over could drink beer, while bars could only serve hard liquor to patrons 21 and over, creating a division in clientele. (Courtesy of Jim Martinson.)

At 1123 East Douglas Avenue, Chance's R, later just known as 1123, and seen here in a later business incarnation, was one of the main hangouts. Visiting the bar, however, was risky since it was located on the city's main thoroughfare and, therefore, highly visible. A popular activity for Wichita youth was "dragging Douglas" at night, meaning that young people had to hurriedly race inside before their peers driving by noticed them. (Courtesy of Dave Quick.)

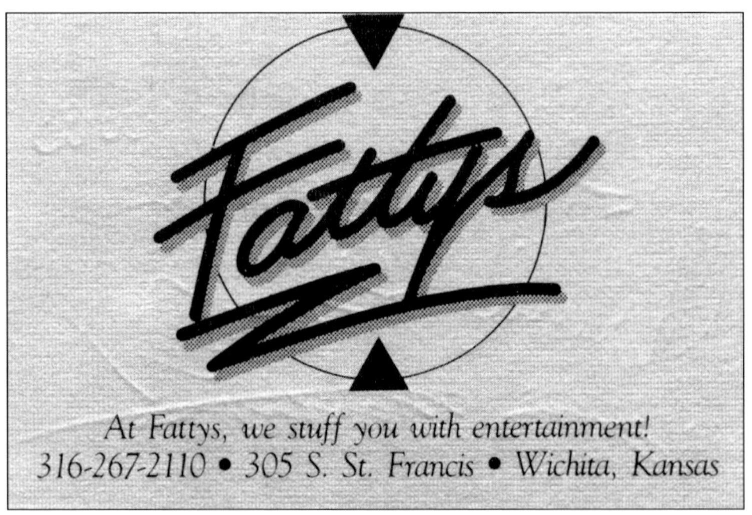

Dudley Toevs summarized the experience of going out to the club as "When you got out of your car and could hear the boom, ba-boom, ba-boom, it said 'you're home, you're home, you're home.'" One of these clubs, Fattys, was located south of Douglas on South St. Francis Street. (Courtesy of Jim Martinson.)

One of the most popular clubs in the late 1970s and early 1980s, the Free Spirit, was located at 410 E. Forty-Seventh Street. With David Wilbur, also known as "Mama Rose," in charge, the club was also known for its internal telephone system, where patrons could call up another table where someone they were interested in was sitting. (Courtesy of Jim Martinson.)

Since clubs and bars were one of the few places people could meet and socialize somewhat openly, different ones catered to different expectations. Zigfield's was intended to be an upscale cocktail lounge as a counterpart to clubs of the time like Lancer's. Mama Rose, of Free Spirit Disco fame, and business partner Greg Harris started the business. (Courtesy of Jim Martinson.)

Sam Winters operated the city's main bathhouse, the Tubs, located at 256-258 North Emporia Avenue, for several years until it closed in the late 1990s. It was known for its themed rooms, such as a jungle room covered in tiki statues and straw wallpaper, and a cave-themed room complete with papier-mâché stalactites and stalagmites. (Courtesy of Wichita-Sedgwick County Historical Museum and Dave Quick.)

By the 1970s, a drag community emerged that, for some, became a surrogate family with figures like Watisha, seen here on the right with Billie Jean Beetem. (Courtesy of Ron Anderson.)

In the 1970s, Jack Hufford was one of the community's best-known bar owners. In the late 1960s, he ran Jack's Jolly Jug on West Second Street and later at 811 S. Chautauqua Street. Later, he opened a club at 1534 South Ida Avenue called "Jack's by the Tracks," due to its proximity to the nearby rail line, it was often jokingly called Jane's by the Trains by the community. Hufford also appeared in a drag persona as "Blanche," below. In addition to drinks and entertainment, Jack's place was known for serving his mother's chili. (Both images courtesy of Jennifer King.)

In the 1970s, Oak Park had become a major hangout for both cruising and socializing. Even those who were simply hanging out got harassed or mugged, and their cars got damaged by "sissy beaters" with little recourse. Going to the police would have just elicited the question, "What were you doing there?" (Both images courtesy of Wichita-Sedgwick County Historical Museum.)

In spite of the risks, Oak Park remained a social hub for years since there were so few other places to meet each other outside of drinking establishments. It was also a place to just hang out and enjoy sunlight and fresh air, as Ron Anderson (left) and Dee Dee Gallegos (right) showed. (Courtesy of Ron Anderson.)

While the main opposition to homosexual rights came from religious leaders, some congregations made the daring choice to support people regardless of orientation. Here, Pastor Bill Reece of Pine Valley Christian Church gives a press conference arguing that Christian love extends to all, including LGBTQ persons. (Courtesy of KAKE-TV and WSU.)

Organized in 1975, Wichita's First Metropolitan Community Church was one of the first congregations specifically open to LGBTQ persons. The congregation moved several times in the 1970s and 1980s, including a church on South Santa Fe Avenue. Here, "Deacon Jimmy" presides in this structure. (Courtesy of Jackie Carter.)

The Wichita State University Homophile Association formed under the leadership of Gary Jo Gardenhire (upper right), Gina Barnett, and Bruce McKinney (center) in 1976 and was recognized by the student government that September. Gardenhire later recalled, "We were a naif, ragtag group full of sass, it was great fun." They joined with the Wichita Gay Community Association and the First Metropolitan Community Church to form the Homophile Association of Sedgwick County (HASC). Together, the members of the HASC lobbied for a nondiscrimination ordinance in 1977. (Courtesy of WSU Spectrum group; quote thanks to an oral history project from Robert Teutsch.)

6A THE WICHITA EAGLE Wednesday, September 28, 1977

Gay Ordinance Passed Despite Threat of Legal Fights

The proposed ordinance was controversial from the start, with proponents saying it provided needed protections and detractors saying it was proof of declining morals. It became part of a national debate in the late 1970s, as progressive changes that had been relatively accepted earlier in the decade, such as the Equal Rights Amendment, had become causes to focus and mobilize conservative voices. (Courtesy of *The Wichita Eagle*.)

In the spring of 1977, HASC endorsed two candidates for the city commission, Connie Peters (above) and Garry Porter (below), in hopes that they would expand the city's civil rights ordinance to include protections for homosexual persons in employment and accommodation. Upon winning the election, the commission embarked on changing the ordinance. Conservative and religious leaders argued aggressively against the ordinance. In spite of the opposition, the commission passed the new ordinance on September 27 by 3-2. The swing vote came from Commissioner Jack Shanahan, who argued his religious faith extended to the protection of all people. (Both images courtesy of Wichita-Sedgwick County Historical Museum.)

REPEAL THE 'GAY RIGHTS' ORDINANCE

VOTE YES FOR REPEAL

Get out and VOTE on May 9, 1978. THE OUTCOME DEPENDS ON EACH ONE OF US.

---

1. **What is the Ordinance we seek to repeal?**
   It is an ordinance passed by the City Commission (by a vote of 3 against 2) which elevates homosexual activity, or other sexual deviation, to a protected, and thereby approved, mode of human conduct.

   The true purpose of the ordinance, and its practical effect, will be to give civic and legal recognition to homosexuality as a legitimate 'lifestyle' which should be accepted in a 'democratic' society.

   There is no doubt about this. The ordinance equates homosexuality with the minorities protected by previously existing civil rights law forbidding discrimination because of race, religion, ethnic origin, etc.

   ----

2. **The Ordinance is unnecessary as far as true rights go.**
   The basic rights of homosexuals have not been violated to any degree that makes such protection by ordinance necessary in the City of Wichita. Wichita is not and has not been a city in which homosexuals exist as a minority suffering in misery, deprived of elemental human existence.

   The record shows that little serious effort was made in all discussion of this ordinance to prove any history of such persecution in this city.

The ordinance empowered conservative leaders like Ron Adrian and Ron Ballard, calling themselves Concerned Citizens for Community Standards of Wichita. They ran a full ad in *The Wichita Eagle* tying homosexuals to child molestation and other crimes. In December, conservative activist Anita Bryant, who had helped Dade County repeal its gay rights ordinance in April 1977, came to Wichita in December 1977 as part of her "Save Our Children" anti-gay crusade. (Above, Courtesy of KAKE-TV and WSU Libraries Department of Special Collections; left, courtesy of Under the Rainbow Oral History Project and the Bruce McKinney Archives, KU.)

Increasing Cloudiness
High. 70s. Low. 50s.

The Wichita Eagle

Despite Alarms, Prof Sleeps Past Job
Story on Page 17A

110 Pages — WICHITA, KANSAS 67201, WEDNESDAY, MAY 10, 1978 — Price 15 Cents

Margin Is More Than 4-to-1

Voters Bury Gay Rights Ordinance

Bryant's and Ballard's campaign worked, Wichita voters approved putting the ordinance on the ballot, and on May 9, 1978, Wichitans repealed the measure by a five to one margin. Gregory Boyd recalled, "It hit us pretty hard and within a few months I and several others left town in disgust; in my case, San Francisco ended up being over a rainbow that was yet to become our national symbol." (Courtesy of *The Wichita Eagle*.)

Gilbert Baker started life in Chanute and Parsons, Kansas. He moved to San Francisco after leaving the military and started sewing banners for anti-war marches. In 1978, city supervisor Harvey Milk requested a unity banner for the Pride parade. Using trash cans to dye long strips of fabric, Baker and others created a giant eight-color flag now recognized worldwide as the original Pride flag. (Courtesy of the *Liberty Press*.)

A builder by profession and talented artist by passion, Linn Copeland emerged as an early community leader. She was active in a wide range of LGBTQ efforts, from supporting other local artists to being active at Metropolitan Community Church and the Kansas Gay Rodeo. Her best-known venture, however, was the bar known as Our Fantasy, founded in 1981 on Hillside and South Thirty-First Streets. A hub of the community for decades, Our Fantasy became the Our Fantasy Complex and was famous for, among so many other things, the Lesbian Luau, the Harbor restaurant, a swimming pool, a duck pond, countless drag shows, and a somewhat easily climbed back fence. Copeland operated it proudly until her passing in 2005. (Left, courtesy of Jennifer King; below, courtesy of Jim Martinson.)

Our Fantasy

Our Fantasy

PRIVATE CLASS B CLUB

3201 S. HILLSIDE ~ WICHITA, KS.

PHONE 682-5494

NAME Jim Martinson

MEMBER'S SIGNITURE

NO. 330 EXPIRES 4/17/82 APPV'D

Linn Copeland remodeled her home along the Arkansas River after a flood, crafting much of the garden and building hardware herself. It eventually became a community hangout in its own right and host of several informal community events. (Courtesy of Jennifer King.)

By the 1980s, a local tradition that emerged was the River Run, where people paddled canoes down to Copeland's home. Here, Fritz Capone poses in front of some canoes. (Courtesy of Jennifer King.)

Born Jimmie Dale Freeman, Fritz Capone had just been crowned Miss Gay Oklahoma when Linn Copeland hired him to perform at the opening of Our Fantasy. He became a fixture as both a bartender and show director. Beyond the bar scene, however, Capone's southern charm and colorful persona were a given at Pride rallies, community events, and charity fundraisers. (Both images courtesy of Jennifer King.)

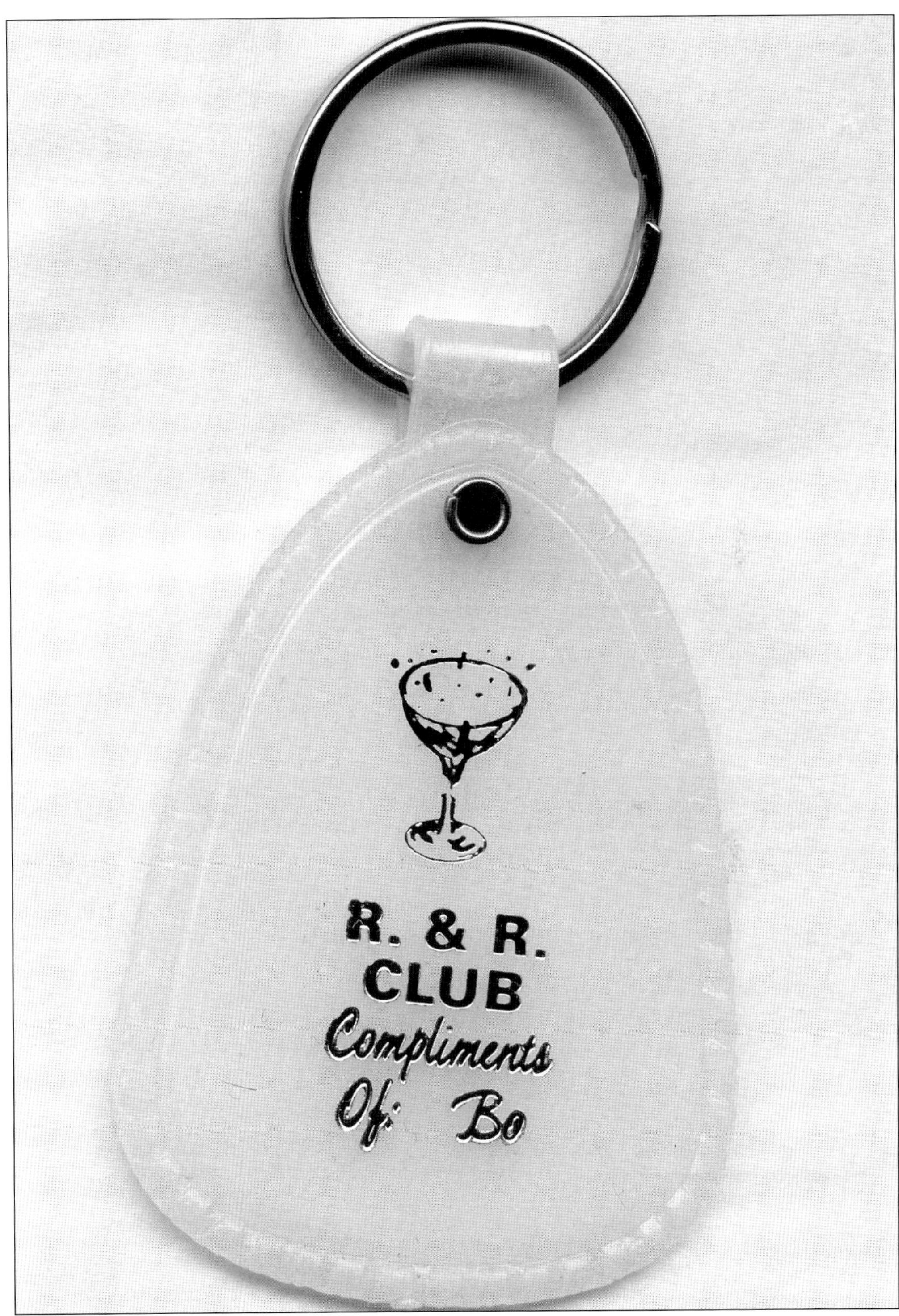

Ray "Bo" Bowe and Ron Tucker initially opened the R & R Brass Rail at 3149 South Lawrence Road before relocating the business to 2828 East Thirty-First Street South, across the street from Our Fantasy. (Courtesy of Jennifer King.)

The R & R became known for its darts, pool events, and shows associated with the Miss Gay Kansas America Pageant. (Courtesy of Jim Martinson.)

While still working for the city, Colleen "Coke" Didier also bartended at places like the R & R and, seen here, Jack's. "Everyone knew Coke when they first came out," King recalled. (Courtesy of Jennifer King.)

Like Linn Copeland's River Run, Bo's Bash was another community gathering event. Here, from left to right, are Jay Caviness, Kolo Kona, and "Bo." (Courtesy of Jennifer King.)

Bo's Bash attracted many community icons. One of these was Danny Olerking, in the center, who was a hairdresser at the Shirkmere Hotel and known for his colorful personality. (Courtesy of Jennifer King.)

Prominent throughout the 1980s and 1990s at Our Fantasy's mainstage shows and on the South Forty's clogging floor, the Rockin' R Cloggers were easily recognizable in their blue denim and white fringe button-ups. Performing in competitions across the state, and nationally, they also hosted dozens of fundraisers, including as part of the Kansas Gay Rodeo Association (KGRA), Fritz's Follies, regional televised competitions, and various community celebrations. (Courtesy of Jennifer King.)

FANTASY

SOUTH FORTY

3201 S. HILLSIDE • WICHITA, KS • 682-5494

Name ____________________

Member's Signature ____________________

No. ________ Expires ________ Appv'd. ________

Named for an old farming reference to the lowest and most remote part of a land section, the South Forty was the local LGBT country western bar, situated directly behind the Our Fantasy Complex. Linked by a thin hallway and shared parking lot, it had its own entrance and access to the pool out back. It was decorated with barrels, wagon wheels, and wood fences and sported a recessed dance floor specifically designed for clogging. It was also the only section of the complex which survived the fire in 1999. (Courtesy of Jennifer King.)

A converted gas station at 2959 South Hillside Street became the home of several bars associated with the leather community. One of the earliest bars at that location was Straps. Then, it was home to JD's, named after the initials of the owners John Melugin and Dusty Rhodes. Boots was there in the mid-1980s. (Courtesy of Jim Martinson.)

Many bar locations changed names and owners over the years. For example, Jack Hufford's club at 1534 South Ida Avenue was Jack's By the Tracks. The location later became the site of Club Tryst, whose logo here was the product of local artist and deejay Kevin Dunn. (Courtesy of the Center of Wichita via Jim Fenton.)

There's no place like home . . . D.J. Kevin Dunn being bussed during his bon voyage party at Kurt's

When HIV first emerged in the news, it was treated by many locals as something happening on the coasts, not in the Midwest. But well-known community members were starting to get sick, like local DJ Kevin Dunn, pictured here. "Going away party" took on a double meaning, and HIV/AIDS sometimes became known as the "homing disease," as people sought familiar surroundings in their final months to say goodbye. Those afflicted faced fear and misunderstanding, and finding doctors was difficult. Social service networks rejected clients, and Wichita's limited resources were even harder to access for those who lived in rural areas. (Both images courtesy of the Center of Wichita and Jim Fenton.)

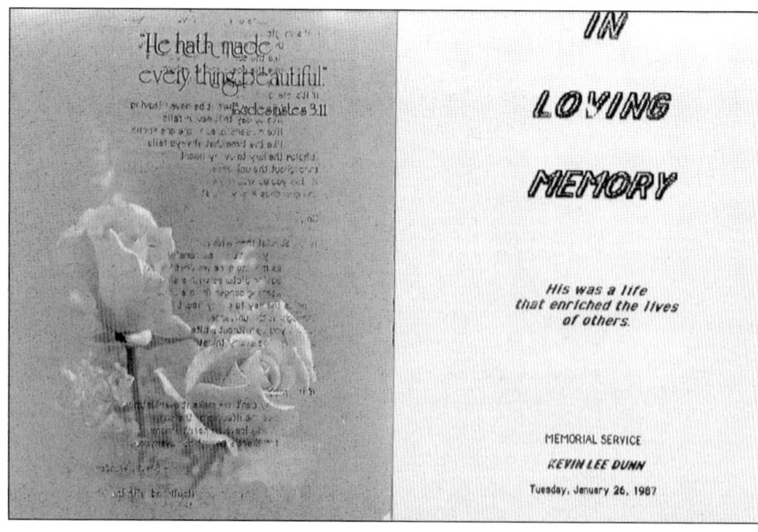

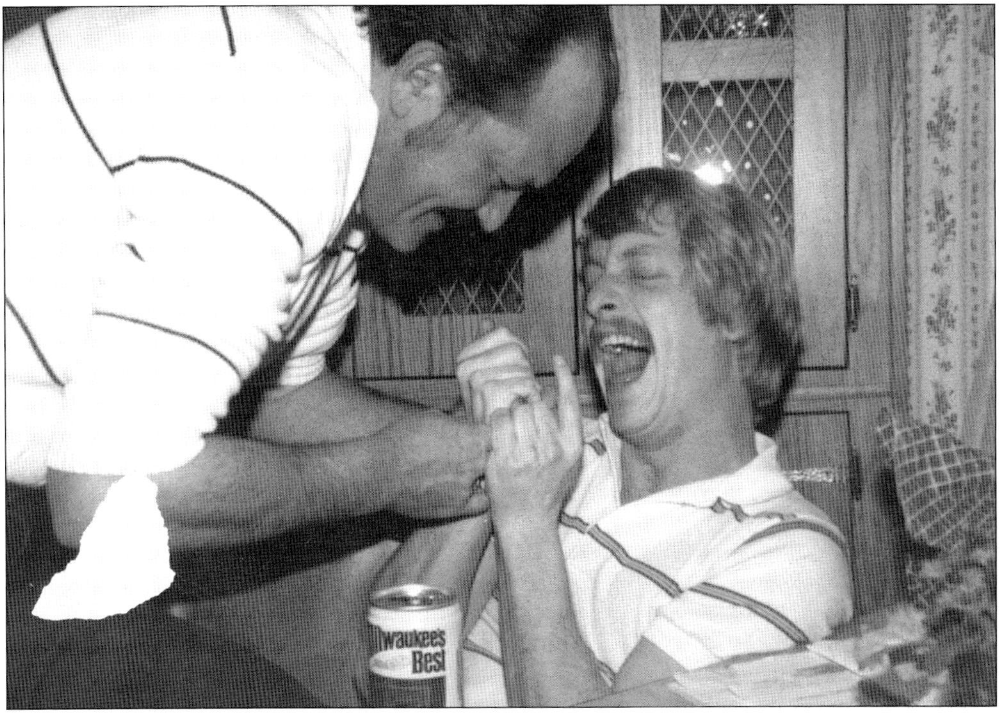

People who suffered from HIV/AIDS faced tremendous discrimination. As late as 1985, despite evidence, the Centers for Disease Control and the American Medical Association were still warning people it might be possible to catch HIV from shared silverware. Some families were fearful of catching it from clothing and personal artifacts, and others were just angry and destroyed personal effects to get rid of them. When Mark Thole got sick, his partner was not even allowed to collect personal items. Instead, Al Tripp created a quilt as a memorial. (Both images courtesy of Virginia Norton.)

The epidemic had arrived. As Martin Mendoza recalled, "You didn't just go to funerals to pay your respects. You went to see who was still here." It also highlighted how few rights couples had who were not married. With the end of life of a partner, a person might find themselves excluded from visiting the hospital, funeral planning, and even being kicked out of their home if the deceased owned the house. (Courtesy of Jennifer King.)

While HIV claimed many public figures, others came back with few connections. Renowned artist Félix Gonzalez-Torres immortalized the experience of many with his 1991 billboard art piece "Untitled" showing nothing but an empty bed. Pastor Jackie Carter remembered, "We were burying them before we even knew their names." (Courtesy of Jennifer King.)

While finishing her residency in 1982, Dr. Donna Sweet began looking into what was then the newly recognized disease of AIDS, and Sweet ended up running one of the most well-known clinics in the country. With longtime associates like case manager Teresa Romey (a former worker with Central Kansas AIDS Project) and performer and fundraiser Fritz Capone, she devoted her career to the treatment of people with HIV/AIDS. She pioneered research and treatment, including being one of the first physicians willing to touch those infected at a time when most physicians wore full-body protective shielding. To help defer the cost of travel and services to those with little money, and as a thank you to her numerous volunteers and associates, Dr. Sweet started hosting Sweet Affair, a yearly gathering at her home. (Right, courtesy of KU School of Medicine; below, courtesy of Dave Quick.)

Fundraisers for Donna Sweet became local events. Among them was the "T Room Review," which brought out both iconic drag queens and those who put on drag just for the event. Above, one of the community's best-known drag performers, Sable, performs. Below, bartender Tom Smiley performs as well. With a demeanor that matched his name, Smiley remained with the bar regardless of changes of names and owners. (Both images courtesy of Virginia Norton.)

In the 1980s, the Metropolitan Community Church congregation purchased the former synagogue of Hebrew Congregation at 156 South Kansas Street. This building served as a meeting space for community groups and social gatherings and a resource for those with HIV/AIDS. Carrying a strong heritage and dating from the 1930s, the building also posed unique challenges for the new congregation, such as the high steps to the main entrance being an obstacle for coffins and attendees during the era's many funerals.

As cases of AIDS rose in the 1980s the need for case management, assisted living, and end-of-life care grew. ConnectCare (CC) was one of the first assistance organizations in Wichita. Former directors included Joe Kelly and Benjamin Klein, who served the community in housing and training medical professionals, and Steven Randall, who was the first certified HIV physician assistant specialist in Kansas. Their assisted living facility, ConnectCare House, closed in 2002 from declining need, with Positive Directions and Dr. Sweet eventually taking on most other services. (Courtesy of Positive Directions.)

Support services became mainstays of the community for years. The Care Coordination Team started in 1991 by Cody Patton, with the help of T. Edward Helms of First Metropolitan Community Church. Patton is on the right at an ArtAID event. From left to right, the others are Molly Brown, Sierra Scott, Marc Durfee, and James Woods. In 2001, the organization changed its name to Positive Directions and later took over some of ConnectCare's services when it closed. (Courtesy of Cody Patton.)

Following the Homophile Association, in 1984, the Gay/Lesbian Resource Association (GLRA) was founded at Wichita State by Doug Glaze together with state delegates, including Steve Wheeler from the Gay/Lesbian Resource Center (GLRC) at K-State and others from the Gay/Lesbian Services of Kansas (GLSK) at the University of Kansas. Glaze approached WSU instructor and counselor LaVona Spencer to be a faculty advisor. After Glaze, Wheeler became president. For three years, the organization hosted campus Pride weeks and weekly social gatherings. (Courtesy of Positive Directions.)

Founded in 1985, Kansans for Dignity, later Kansans for Human Dignity, became an early organization for LGBTQ rights by hosting events, advocacy talks, and other activities. In the early 1990s, the organization, under the leadership of Bruce McKinney, Kristi Parker, Jim Fenton, and Cyndi Cook, among others, founded the first incarnation of The LGBT Center of Wichita. Opened on March 6, 1994, it was located at 111 Spruce Avenue, just down the street from East High. (Courtesy of KU).

A Pride rally in the 1990s in front of the county courthouse features a section of the rainbow flag. (Courtesy of Jennifer King.)

Three

From Cowtown to Gaytown

We were gay before it was cool.

—*Liberty Press*

The LGBTQ community established a number of key centers of support. Pride emerged as a central event of the year, while the Kansas Gay Rodeo held events and the community worked to commemorate the 25th anniversary of Stonewall. Along Thirty-First Street stood a complex of businesses adjacent to Our Fantasy and the South Forty. This was the time when drag queens such as Big Mama Simone and Fritz Capone reigned supreme. Meanwhile, organizations such as PFLAG supported youth and their families, while Positive Directions served the needs of those with HIV/AIDS. Churches and religious organizations advocated hosted worship and social events even as issues of inclusion raged within many traditions. The Wichita Center developed as an important resource, while the *Liberty Press* became a regional chronicle of events, people, and resources. That said, challenges persisted. Hostile protests from Westboro Baptist Church became expected parts of events and celebrations. Growing public acceptance appeared in popular culture, while President Clinton diminished hopes for LGBTQ military service. A growing LGBTQ business community of professionals and business owners emerged, some embracing their role as community leaders and others wary that too much visibility might be challenging among their clients and patrons in the larger community. Even so, the turn of a new century and new millennium brought both hopes for change and anxiety for what was next.

D. 85729

Articles of Incorporation

1-30-84
857292

We, the undersigned, incorporators, hereby associate ourselves together to form and establish a corporation *NOT* for profit under the laws of the State of Kansas.

FIRST: The Name of the Corporation is Wichita Gay Community Pride Committee, Incorporated.

000001 10 6571 01-23-84
9 ARTICLES INC. 1 50.0
10 TRANS. TOTAL 1 50.0

SECOND: The location of its registered office in Kansas is 1704 South Sante Fe, Wichita Sedgwick 67211
(Number) (Street) (City) (County) (Zip Code)

and the resident agent in charge thereof at such address is Rev. Bob Twar

THIRD: This Corporation is organized *NOT* for profit and the nature of its business or purposes to be conducted or promoted is: to stimulate and acknowledge pride among the gay community, and advance its awareness to society. The objectives to be used in seeking these goals are Education, Social Interaction, Political awareness and Social Justice, and to accept donations and raise funds and disburse them for the aforesaid purpose.

FOURTH: This corporation shall not have authority to issue capital stock.

The total number of shares of this corporation is as follows:

Formed in 1981 and officially incorporated in 1984, the Wichita Gay Community Pride Committee emerged as a board distinct from other community organizations and businesses with the specific purpose of organizing Pride Fest. A social event only, Pride Fest was distinct from rallies, which were explicitly political in nature.

In 1988, the Wichita Gay Community Pride Committee became The Wichita Gay/ Lesbian Alliance (WGLA). An association of organizations, the alliance came to include groups such as Berdache, Cathedral of the Plains, First Metropolitan Community Church, Kansans for Human Dignity, the Kansas Gay Rodeo Association, PFLAG, and the Wichita Transgender Alliance. (Courtesy of Jim Martinson.)

Agenda

Call to order

1. Opening. Moderator.

2. Member Organizations, remarks

a. Berdache
b. Fantasy Complex
c. First Metropolitan Community Church
d. Kansas Gay Rodeo Association
e. Responsible Active Gays

3. Committees

a. Gay And Lesbian Awards
b. Wichita Pride Committee
c. Womens Committee

4. Organizations Invited to speak

a. ACT UP/Wichita
b. A.I.D.S. Referal Services
c. ConnectCare - Hospice
d. Gay Services Bureau
e. Land of Awes BBS
f. Mission of Faith Fellowship
g. Wichita Police Liason - Cindy Tade
h. significant others

5. Community Members Concerns

Question & Answer Session,
for organizations & persons present

One of the key annual community events throughout the 90s and into the 2000s was the Gay and Lesbian Awards (GALA). Eventually, the Gay/Lesbian Alliance disbanded, but the awards banquet, including recognition of Wichita mayor Elma Broadfoot, left, continued for years afterward. The last GALA was held as part of a week of events for Pride Fest 2012 on the top floor of what is now the Red Roof Inn on East Kellogg Drive. (Courtesy of Jennifer King.)

Minister Fred Phelps of Topeka, Kansas, is depicted here as the famous horror character Freddy Kreuger, even featuring fake blood splattered across the poster. Phelps was one of America's most active anti-gay protestors, leading the congregation of Westboro Baptist Church. Phelps and the congregation frequently protested at the funerals of HIV/AIDS patients and at military funerals, believing that God was punishing the United States for its tolerance of homosexuality. (Courtesy of KU.)

1996 Rainbow FESTIVAL OF THE ARTS

Gay/Lesbian Video Showcase Series

Beginning **June 16th**, and continuing through the end of the month, an unusual collection of films will be seen -- **most for the first time EVER in the state of Kansas.**

Eighteen (18) films from eight (8) different countries have been specially selected to show how Gays and Lesbians are depicted on-screen globally. The series includes specially selected programs dealing with historically significant issues creating a **one-of-a-kind festival** that truly has something for everyone.

All presentations are free of charge, but seating is limited and offered on a first-come basis. All showtimes are at **7:30pm** unless otherwise posted and will be presented at The Center, **111 N. Spruce.**

Remember: if you don't see these films during the Showcase Series, you probably won't see them at all ... because they simply aren't to be found at your local video store.
Don't miss out!!

Film Highlights ...

The Loved One [1965] [G] USA Brilliant farce with Robert Morse cast as an English poet/plagiarist who comes to Hollywood, where he's introduced to the ritual of the American funeral after his uncle commits suicide.

Gay Themes on TV Sitcoms [1981-95] [G] USA A collection of prime-time TV sitcoms culled from the Berdache video archives. Four full-length episodes will be shown chosen from a list that includes: MASH, Golden Girls, Roseanne, Friends, Murphy Brown, and Seinfeld.

Urinal [1988] [NR] Canada Audacious satire in which a group of dead gay artists come together in an effort to research the policing of washroom sex in Toronto! In addition, Dorian Gray takes on the role of an undercover agent, and infiltrates the police force.

more on back cover ...

Law of Desire [1986] [NR] Spain Another outrageous comedy from Pedro Almodovar, which tells of a love-obsessed gay Madridian and his transsexual brother/sister, among others, getting hopelessly entangled in cross-gender relationships.

The 4th Man [1984] [NR] Denmark Paul Verhoeven's stylish thriller about an alcoholic homosexual writer, and his rather vivid hallucinations and fantasies.

Last Call at Maud's [1993] [NR] USA Illuminating documentary which centers around the closing of Maud's, the oldest lesbian bar in San Francisco: an event which serves to mirror the changing lesbian scene in both the city and the nation.

Taxi Zum Klo [1981] [NR] Germany At once lauded and condemned upon its release, this controversial in-your-face film tells the story of a gay teacher who is in conflict with his lover; he begins cruising public bathrooms, in search of fast and easy sex. NOTE: This film contains scenes of graphic sexuality.

The Center Presents ...

An Evening With Tracey Hughes

Enjoy Tracey's celebrated trip through Black Women's Culture.

June 14th
8:00 pm 111 N. Spruce

The Berdache Archive is hosting the creation of a Video History Project, featuring the **"Stories of Our Lives."**

Video History/Herstory Project

JUNE 13 **8:00 PM**

The evening begins with the showcasing of a History Project Video, and ends with the audience participating in the creation of their own Video History Project.

Join in on this unique historical experience!!!

BERDACHE

111 N. SPRUCE

KC's Closet Fashion Show

A show to benefit the ***Northern Lights Alternative***. Fashions will be supplied by KC's Closet. Show begins shortly after Tracey's performance. Don't miss this!!

June 14th

As this brochure noted, "The Rainbow Festival of the Arts was an ambitious—and well-received—week of events at Wichita's first Gay Community Center that included stage productions, readings, a fashion show, and the initial oral history video tapings of the Berdache 'Stories of our Lives' project." (Courtesy of Gregory Boyd.)

Held on the 20th anniversary of Stonewall, Pride Fest 1989 featured T-shirts, like the one below, and $3 bills (from the joke "queer as a $3 bill") used to purchase Pride shirts or food plates at the event. Anti-gay singer Anita Bryant appeared on the front of the bill with the Wichita skyline on the back, graced by the phrase "In Gay We Trust," hanging over the famous downtown landmarks of the Wichita Holiday Inn and Century II. (Both images courtesy of the Center of Wichita and Jim Fenton.)

Although Pride events had been part of community life for years, the first combined Pride parade and rally took place in June 1990. It divided the community. Activists sought greater visibility, but many others, remembering the hostility of the 1978 anti-discrimination vote just 12 years earlier, feared violence. As one community member noted, "It might do some good, but I don't have the guts to do it." Gregory Boyd had been part of the parade's planning, and his footage became the basis of a film documentary about the event shown above. Within a year, citywide Pride festivals with printed guidebooks marked a more visible phase. (Both images courtesy of the Center of Wichita, Jim Fenton, and Gregory Boyd.)

What made 1991's Pride different was how open it was, taking place down Main Street in public view. Here, members of First Metropolitan Church near Second and Main Streets, with the city's historic Occidental Hotel in the background. (Courtesy of Jennifer King and Ron Anderson.)

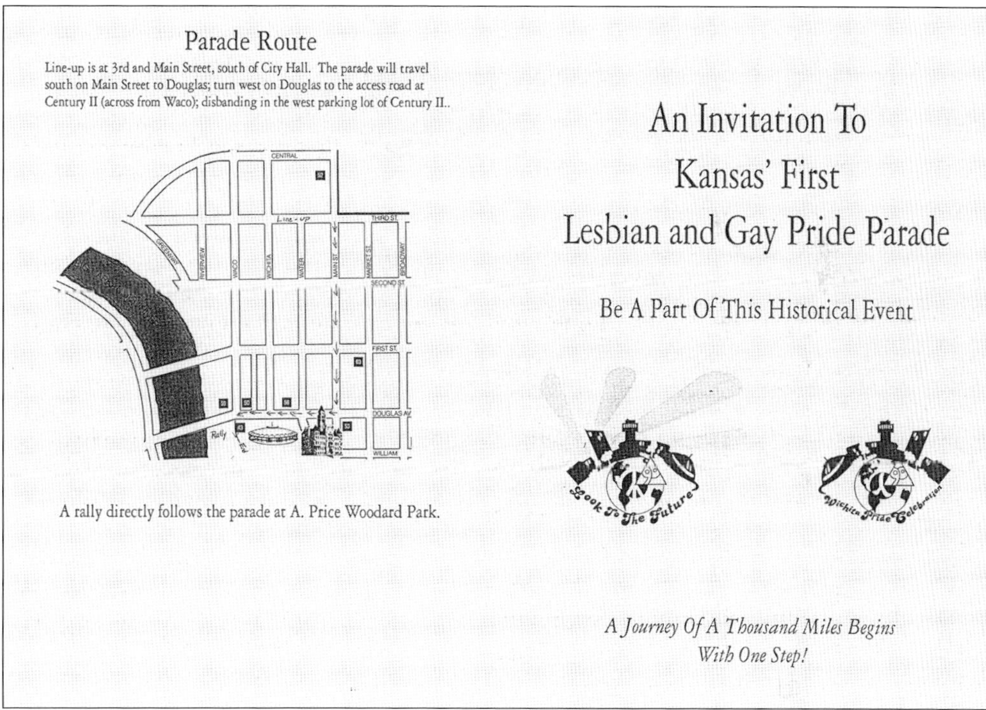

Being open, with a parade on one of the city's main streets and a publicized route, was a significant risk. Club owners were often among the wariest, concerned Pride events might attract public hostility. In the background was the fear that protests could use the route information to plan organized attacks. As a result, the path was often mapped deliberately to maximize visibility but minimize surprises. (Courtesy of KU.)

Naming the community became a complicated issue as well. "Gay" had come to be accepted mainly for men. Many women called themselves lesbian, while others still called themselves gay, and still, others simply used the term "butch." Those with a more activist bent wanted to reclaim the term "queer," but for most, the name still had a pejorative meaning. Combining the terms was also a challenge, as some felt starting with "gay" prioritized men. By the 1990s, "Les-Bi-Gay," and later "Les-Bi-Gay-Trans," was becoming a more used term. (Courtesy of the *Liberty Press*.)

During the mid-90s, the Pride march coincided with Gay Rodeo and included a march from the courthouse to Old Cowtown Museum, pictured here. This route was repeated for Pride Fest 2012. (Courtesy of Jennifer King.)

Many Pride events in the 1990s and early 2000s took place in Naftzger Park, ironically the site of the 1960s Beat hangout Moody's Skidrow Beanery. (Courtesy of Jennifer King.)

Seated in Linn Copeland's red truck at an early Pride march, Fritz Capone rides in full regalia. The celebrations took place with both a celebration and a tone of fear. "We were worried," said Jennifer King. "We did not know if any attacks would take place." (Courtesy of Jennifer King.)

Although the community thinks of Wichita Pride as a continuous entity, it has gone through several incarnations. The Pride Alliance from the 1980s ceased to function for a few years, but by the 1990s, the organization revived. Pride Fest in 1995 included a major event at the then West Bank Stage of the Arkansas River. Deb Davis, one of the organizers, seen above, then traveled to San Diego, below, where the San Diego Pride leaders helped guide efforts in Wichita. (Both images courtesy of Deb Davis and Staci Steddum.)

At Wichita State, Glaze's Gay/Lesbian Resource Association (formerly the Student Homophile Association) became incorporated into Students for Education on Liberal Concerns (SELC) from 1987 to 1988. It became Responsible Active Gays (RAG) in 1989. From 1991 to 1992 it was renamed to Choices, and from 1992 to 1993, it was Club Alternative, settling on the name Ten Percent (a reference to LGBTQ being 10 percent of the population) in 1994. (Courtesy of WSU Spectrum group and Medford Logsdon.)

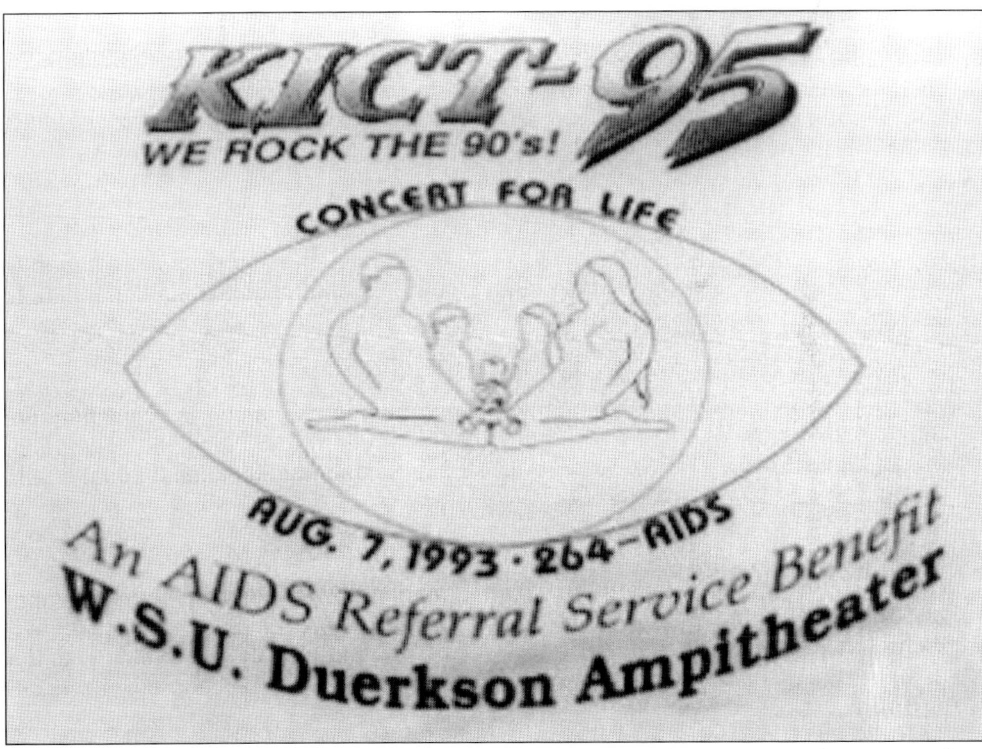

In 1993, the WSU Student Government refused Ten Percent its charter, stating the group violated Kansas sodomy law. Co-president Kim Card and vice president Catherine Boyle appealed. Their appeal was granted. That same year, local rock radio station KICT-95 hosted the "We Rock the 90s: Concert for Life" at WSU's Duerksen Amphitheater. It featured Painted Saint, Danger Bros, and Dead Orchestra, and proceeds were donated to AIDS Referral Service (ARS) on South Broadway. (Courtesy of WSU Spectrum group.)

EMERALD CITY News

PUBLISHED BY
THE LAND OF AWES INFORMATION SERVICES
ISSUE #10
SEPTEMBER, 1989

ECN FEATURE

National Coming Out Day

OCTOBER 11-1989

On October 11th, millions of gay Americans will observe the second annual "National Coming Out Day." Although the event is a month away, local and national organizers are preparing various activities to draw attention to what this day means and the benefits that can emerge from taking just one simple step outward to ourselves, our community and our nation. The event relies primarily on the willingness of local groups to plan and carry out events that support individuals to take their next step in "coming out".

Last year, the first year for National Coming Out Day, the event received widespread media attention to include coverage in USA Today, CNN, National Public Radio, This Way Out and the Oprah Winfrey Show.

The Emerald City News conducted three interviews with the individuals who are working as chairpersons and national coordinator for the October event. The National Coming Out Day headquarters are located in Santa Fe New Mexico.

Pilo Bueno is the National Coordinator for National Coming Out Day, a year round position that is especially busy, May through October. Bueno provided *Emerald City News* with information concerning the structure of the organization, as well information on how individuals and organizations can become a part of the national event.

"National Coming Out Day is incorporated in New Mexico and we have filed our 501 (C)(3) with the federal government, which we should receive soon. Last year, National Coming Out Day was a project of National Gay Rights Advocates, run together with "The Experience" workshops. The project originated at the

IN THIS ISSUE...

In late 1988, Rex Rivers's Land of Awes printing company launched one of the community's earliest newsletters, *Emerald City News*, which included local information but was especially focused on national issues such as HIV/AIDS topics and legal and political news. (Courtesy of Jim Martinson.)

Kansas Alternative Press

Volume 1 Issue 1 August 4, 1989

HOPE OR HOAX?

by Tami Bassett

Walking for A.I.D.S. to raise money for World Health Organization (W.H.O.)and local A.I.D.S. organizations, this was what Mr. Bill Mole had said he was doing when he came to Wichita in mid-June to promote his walking. He was given special permission from one bar owner only if the ambassadors would know how much money was raised and that it was given to the local organizations. Before he departed, The community had reach in and given some so that a better tomorrow would happen for all of us.

Upon his arrival in Kansas City a bar owner asked Gary Johnson a member of ACT UP/KC to do some research on Bill Mole and his walk around the world. Gary called and spoke with Anna Verda who is representative of W.H.O. in New York. They had received a check in June of '88 and the next time they heard anything was September of 1988 when they received a 1989 itinerary. The itinerary that W.H.O. had placed him in West Germany when he was in kansas City. W.H.O. also said that he had no direct permission from them to solicit money. Later that evening when questioned about money Bill said that he had given $450.00 dollars to W.H.O. when asked if he had permission from the organization to solicit money, he presented a courtesy letter and said he would have to give $100,000 before they would endorse him. He was also Questioned about financial statements which he was unable to provide or a non-profit license. When asked about his visa he said it was a visitors visa. When

CONT. ON PAGE 10

In 1988, Tami J. Bassett was in the process of returning to Wichita from Las Vegas and conceived a news outlet to parallel that of *Emerald City News.* In August 1989, *Kansas Alternative News* released its first edition. The publication ran for a few months before an accident claimed Bassett's life. (Courtesy of Jim Martinson.)

Most larger cities had various cheap or free independent publications. Known as "zines" (and in the gay community, sometimes jokingly called "fag rags"), they announced local events and news and advertised gay-friendly businesses and organizations. Along with *Emerald City News* and *Kansas Alternative News* in the late 1980s, others joined in the early 1990s, including the Gay/Lesbian Alliance's *Signals*, the *Parachute*, and the *Triangle*. (Courtesy of the Center of Wichita and Jim Fenton.)

Started by Kristi Parker and Vinnie Reed in 1994, and in continuous print until Kristi's unexpected passing in 2018, the *Liberty Press* was Wichita's longest-running and most popular LGBTQ publication. It was distributed for free to most of the community bars and social support organizations, it was also the primary Pride guide for Pride Fest most years. (Courtesy of the Center of Wichita and Kristi Parker.)

Bear News

Wichita Bears
P.O.Box 16751
Wichita, KS 67216

1(888)MAN-BEAR
1(888)626-2327
http://www.bear.net/clubs/wichita.bears/

April, 1997, Volume II, Issue 10

April 3-6 TEXAS BEAR ROUND-UP Dallas TX

Here We COME!!

BEARS IN PAJAMAS

Dubbed Another Success

By Randy W.

Saturday March 22, 1997 The Wichita Bears were joined by the Junction City Teddy Bears at The Sidesteet Saloon for a fur filled evening of bears running around in their night clothes. I don't think I've seen that many hot men in one room since the Dallas Bear Round-up in 1996. WOOF!!!

Several of the Wichita Bears volunteered their culinary expertise by preparing for a chili feed. Dinner was enjoyed by all in the club, bears or not (bears helped themselves to everyone...I mean...everything in sight!). Mike Sullivan procured the equipment to provide music for the evening. He's one hell of a DJ who knows how to keep a party going! Thanks Mike.

Continued on page 2.

Along with Peejays, Chili was served up by the 'Bears.

Wichita Bears PICNIC!
Sunday 1:00 pm
April 20 – Zoo Park
Bring a picnic lunch!
April 27 – Business Meeting
Vince & Randy's

Executive Council:	Warren Gordon
	Randy Whisnant
	Jim Wildman
Recording Secretary	Jack Kraus (acting)
Corresponding Secretary:	Mike Sullivan
Accounting:	Robert K.

Wichita Bears' Bear News is published monthly except January and July. Subscription rate is $10 per year (make check or money order payable to Kent Enterprises). Subscription Wichita Bears c/o Mike Sullivan, P.O.Box 16751, Wichita, KS 67216. All articles and submissions become property of Wichita Bears and are copyrighted; all rights reserved; nothing may be reproduced without written permission, with the exception of event schedules.

In contrast to the gay community's focus on fit and toned youth, the bear movement celebrated the range of body types from slim to heavy with a particular focus on men who had facial and body hair. In Wichita, groups like Hirsute Pursuit brought bears together for both social events as well as community fundraisers and even had their own newsletter, shown below. (Both images courtesy of Jim Martinson.)

Recognizing many Native American tribes had unique ideas of gender and sexuality, early French and Spanish conquistadors documented them under the collective term "berdache" ("bear-*dash*-eh"). This history was repopularized in the 1970s as part of the broader men's movement. Berdache societies formed in several cities over the years, including one in Wichita by local artists and activists, including Cindi Cook, Gregory Boyd, and Bruce McKinney. Due to its offensive origin, the term "berdache" fell out of favor, and several US and Canadian Native groups coined "two-spirit" in the 1990s to distance themselves from European terminology. Two HIV/AIDS coordinators at Hunter Health Clinic, Pam Harjo and Michael St. Claire, formed the Wichita Two-Spirit Council in the mid-2000s to support LGBTQ individuals of Native descent. It was renamed the Two-Spirit Society in 2012 and has been headed by Brent Kennedy since 2014. (Above, courtesy of the Center of Wichita; below, courtesy of Brent Kennedy.)

BERDACHE

is committed to:

- Educating the general public, health care professionals and those at high risk
- Preventing disease and Promoting health
- Providing vital support services to people with AIDS (PWAs), their families and loved ones.

Liberty Press

Volume 9, No. 10 • June 2003
www.libertypress.net

Rainbow Flag Turns 25

Original designer Gilbert Baker, a native Kansan, restores flag to original design

PLUS, PRIDE IN KANSAS!
Check out what's going on for Pride week in Topeka and Wichita!

Proudly Serving Lesbian & Gay Kansans Since 1994

In 1994, commemorating the 25th anniversary of the Stonewall Uprising and march, Gilbert Baker was commissioned to create a mile-long version of his original rainbow Pride flag. This new version eliminated the pink and turquoise stripes due mainly to the cost of the dye. Following the march, that flag was cut into one-foot-wide sections and donated to organizations all over the world. As a result, it has become the basis for the now highly recognizable modern six-stripe rainbow Pride flag. One donation recipient was Wichita's own Kristi Parker, who subsequently donated it to the Center of Wichita's archive.

When Josh Shepler got harassed at school, his mother, Mary Shepler, who worked for the district court human resources office, pushed for support for student protection. After being told her son should expect some degree of bullying, she pushed the case to the Kansas Supreme Court. As a response, Josh was featured on *Oprah* in 1996 to talk about school harassment. This started a career in theater and drama in New York. On his return home, he said in the *Liberty* Press, "I have grown from a loud-mouthed Wichitan to a loud-mouthed Brooklynite." (Courtesy of the *Liberty Press*.)

Fear of HIV/AIDS merged with attitudes about homosexuality in general. In Kansas, a proposed Senate Bill 287 would have made it illegal for an HIV-positive person to engage in physical acts. Given the lack of response and outright hostility to the community in general and those with HIV/AIDS in particular, the AIDS Coalition To Unleash Power or ACT UP emerged in 1990 to engage in more activist tactics and bring about public awareness of the issue. (Courtesy of KU.)

By the 1990s, Kellogg Avenue had become an informal place of public discourse as groups and people placed signs and messages on walking bridges that crossed the highway for passing motorists to read. In 1990, local ACT UP activists placed a "Silence=Death" banner on the walking bridge. The city removed it later that morning. (Courtesy of WSU.)

In the 1970s, a gay rodeo movement developed that featured some of the standard events along with unique competitions such as "goat dressing." The movement came to Wichita in 1986 when Linn Copeland brought to town Fritz Capone, who had been the newly crowned Miss Oklahoma Gay Rodeo. A Kansas Gay Rodeo chapter soon followed, the sixth in the country. In 1989, Linn Copeland became president of the International Gay Rodeo Association. (Both images courtesy of Jennifer King.)

In October 1991, it was Kansas's turn to host the gay rodeo, an event that happened to coincide with the International Gay Rodeo Finals. However, this big opportunity almost did not take place. When the owner of the original location learned that it was a gay event, they backed out. Quick work on the part of Linn Copeland and supportive city officials relocated the event to the west bank of the Arkansas River, right downtown. (Right, courtesy of Jim Martinson; below, courtesy of Jennifer King.)

The NAMES Project AIDS Memorial Quilt began in 1987 as a piece of folk art by Cleve Jones in San Francisco. By 1991, the quilt had over 14,000 individual panels, and sections were touring the country. Part of that tour was a display in Wichita at Century II in December, sponsored by the special committee *A Commitment to Care*. That same year, the International Gay Rodeo Association named the quilt their rodeo grand marshal. (Courtesy of Jim Martinson.)

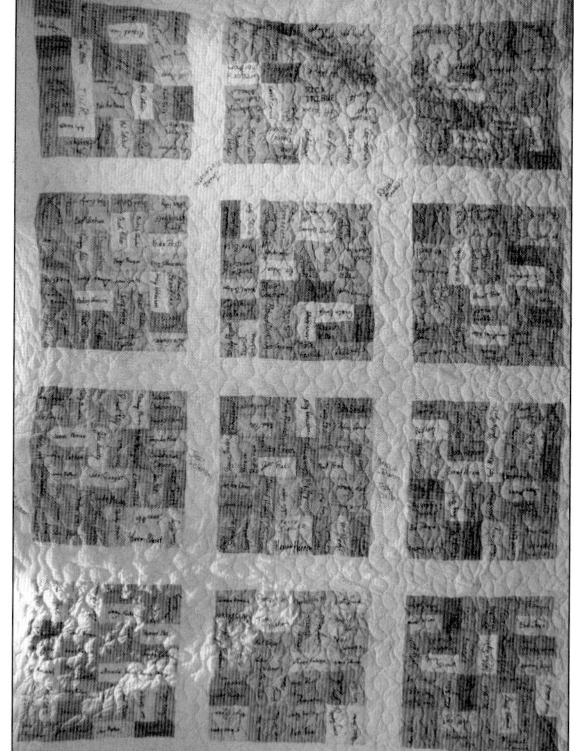

The quilt prompted local versions, including this one for Wichita. Created in the 1990s, this quilt lists the names of those locally with HIV/AIDS whom Positive Directions served. (Courtesy of the Center of Wichita.)

The NAMES Project Quilt returned to Wichita in May 1997 and was sponsored by the Wichita Quilt Host Committee, which included several local organizations. Panels were draped throughout the building and across the floor and were still only a small section of the overall piece. Despite the large crowds the hall was noticeably quiet. (Both images courtesy of Jennifer King.)

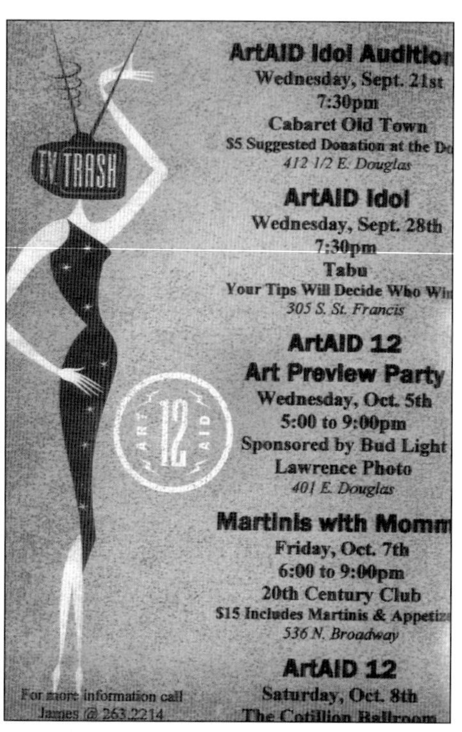

Nearly as old as the AIDS Walk-Run, ArtAID was a creation of Planet Hair Salon as a benefit for the ConnectCare Community AIDS Program, starting in 1993. Originally a single-night dinner and show with an art auction, ArtAID eventually grew into a multi-day extravaganza. It also became a primary resource for Positive Directions and the Sweet Emergency Fund, with sold-out shows and dozens of donated works in a variety of mediums. Planet Hair ended involvement in 2013, and the event was discontinued three years later. (Courtesy of Positive Directions.)

Started in Harlem in 1989 by Pernessa Seele, the National Week of Prayer for the Healing of AIDS (NWPHA) was an encouragement for love, support, and destigmatization of those with HIV/AIDS in traditionally Black congregations. It led to the now international organization Balm in Gilead, Inc., and works with the Care Coordination Team in Kansas. From left to right are (front row) Pastor Lincoln Montgomery, Rev. Wanda-Gail Logan, and Pastor Kevass Harding; (second row) Pastor Willard Dallas, Dr. Donna Sweet, and Dr. Tony Ross. (Courtesy of Positive Directions.)

When Fritz Fiedler died of AIDS in 1991, his mother, Bev, threw herself into activism on behalf of the cause of HIV and AIDS persons. Not long after Fritz's passing, Fiedler received an invitation from Marilee Harper to help form the Wichita Chapter of the Parents and Friends of Gay Persons or PFLAG. Until her passing in 2006, Bev was a champion for PFLAG, coordinating events and staffing the group's helpline. (Courtesy of the *Liberty Press*.)

Beginning with her joining PFLAG and eventually rising to chairwoman of their member council, Sally Morse has been a tireless activist and ally for the community in Wichita since the 1980s. She was a founding member of the original Wichita LGBT Center, and the first official librarian of the current center, which was dedicated in her honor in 2018, pictured here. (Courtesy of the Center of Wichita.)

Oak Park had long been an LGBTQ hangout. Periodically, the sign OAK PARK was informally changed to GAY PARK, changing the "O" to a "G" and the "K" to "Y." When the city decided to install frisbee golf in the park, in part to discourage gay activity, a group called the Slut Puppies formed their own frisbee team to continue meeting there. (Courtesy of Jim Martinson.)

When the bar Cruisin' opened, the "Slut Puppies" was a "disorganized group" consisting of Tim McMaster, Tim McCullough, Bill Swift, and Jim Martinson welcomed new patrons and encourage them to keep coming back. In time, this "sex positive" club partnered with other groups, such as those with the leather and bear communities, to hold cross-over events. (Courtesy of Jim Martinson.)

Returning to Wichita after living in California, Raye Ann Tucker and Renee Fletcher found a lack of venues to get LGBTQ merchandise and books. Rather than just ordering items from out of state, the pair opened one of the city's first LGBTQ bookstores, Visions and Dreams, at 3143 West Maple Street in 1993. (Courtesy of Deb Davis and Staci Steddum.)

Gene, known locally as "Mother," opened Mother's Cards, Mags & Gifts in the 1990s as one of the only specifically LGBT-oriented gift shops in the region. Located across the street from Our Fantasy/South Forty, his store was a fixture of the community for over a decade, offering everything from Pride flag jewelry to LGBT greeting cards, magazines, and films. He regularly donated his space and his time to individuals in need and several local organizations, including PFLAG, Positive Directions, and advertising in the *Liberty Press*. Closing the shop in the early 2000s, he passed in 2022. (Courtesy of Dawn Harris.)

A member of the Kiowa Nation, Spencer Guoladdle was better known in the community as "Big Mama Simone." As much a fixture in the community as Fritz or Linn, Big Mama could often be found hosting shows at Fantasy and South Forty, partying at fundraisers, and laughing out on the patio by the Fantasy pool. (Courtesy of Virginia Norton.)

Ron Anderson was an unassuming person whose main efforts involved community work with Pride and being a leader at Metropolitan Community Church. Pressured to try drag at Free Spirit back in 1980, Anderson won the crown as Miss Mardi Gras Emeritus. By the 2000s, Anderson's alter ego had become the vivacious and spirited Candace Capri, winning the Miss Queen of Hearts contest in 2003. (Courtesy of Ron Anderson.)

The "Fantasy Follies" included the performers Rusty Franklin, Fritz Capone, Watisha De Williams, and Sahdji. (Courtesy of Jennifer King.)

Richard Brown recalled, "When I created Cypress, it was basically to get into the crowd at the Fantasy. I wanted to be one of the popular girls. And then I got involved in rodeo, which was something unusual for a black drag queen. . . . But it seemed to do the trick and then I crossed over into the pageantry." Her photograph now appears proudly at J's Lounge. (Courtesy of Richard Brown and J's Lounge.)

Some drag was about fun and parody, especially when it came to fundraising efforts. Here, Tommy Morrison performs as Sibyl Louise Coochbottom as part of the "Wrinkle Room" Pageant at the R & R Brass Rail. (Courtesy of Jennifer King.)

Side Street Saloon opened in 1994 and was located on South Pattie Street in the middle of an older residential neighborhood, well away from the Thirty-First Street hub. (Courtesy of the *Liberty Press*.)

In the 1990s, figures like Phil Speary promoted plays on gay topics at places like the Wichita Community Theater with the goal that "if we want to do this, then let's do it right." After leading plays at venues such as Theater on Consignment, Speary launched the Guild Hall Players at St. James Episcopal Church in 2006. Not all of the productions are LBGTQ-focused, but figures like Speary helped the community support productions that would have been uncomfortably controversial just a few decades earlier. (Courtesy of Phil Speary.)

Many aspects of the local art and performance scene were LGBTQ-friendly, if not specifically, LGBTQ establishments. One of these was a cabaret venue in downtown Wichita that was initially called Roxy's, and then Christine Tasheff opened Cabaret Old Town in that space in 1993. In 2014, a group of theater supporters purchased the business and renamed it Roxy's in honor of that previous name. (Courtesy of Benjamin and Curtis Breese-Isley.)

Through the 1990s, Wichita's LGBTQ clubs were on the city's southern edges, with Thirty-First Street being a major corridor. However, by the 2000s, a series of new clubs appeared downtown, including the Metro at Central and Waco. Located next to both city hall and the county courthouse, the Metro represented a shift in attitude, where clubs could be located near centers of government and law enforcement. It also frequently featured paid dancers like Colton Haynes, who eventually starred in the television show *Teen Wolf*. (Courtesy of the *Liberty Press*.)

Having left Wichita, Jim "Jay" Basham lived in places like Oregon and Las Vegas, only to return to Wichita in 1998 with his partner. In 2001, he opened J's Lounge on Central Avenue. Even so, the legacy of needing to be hidden and out of sight persisted. Some customers only entered and left through the side door so as not to be seen on Central.

By the late 1980s, Jack Hufford was ready to step away from the bar business and sold the bar at 1507 Pawnee Street that had become Toto's, a club that Nelson Stump owned between 1989 and 1992. In the 1990s, Jack's partner, Howard Harville, seen here on the left, renamed it the T-Room. After Hufford's death in 1999 and Harville's move to Florida, it became the location for other bars, including Trends and 1507. (Courtesy of Jennifer King.)

T-Room's bartender Jeff Siroky is pictured here with Charles Conzales as Caliente. (Courtesy of Virginia Norton.)

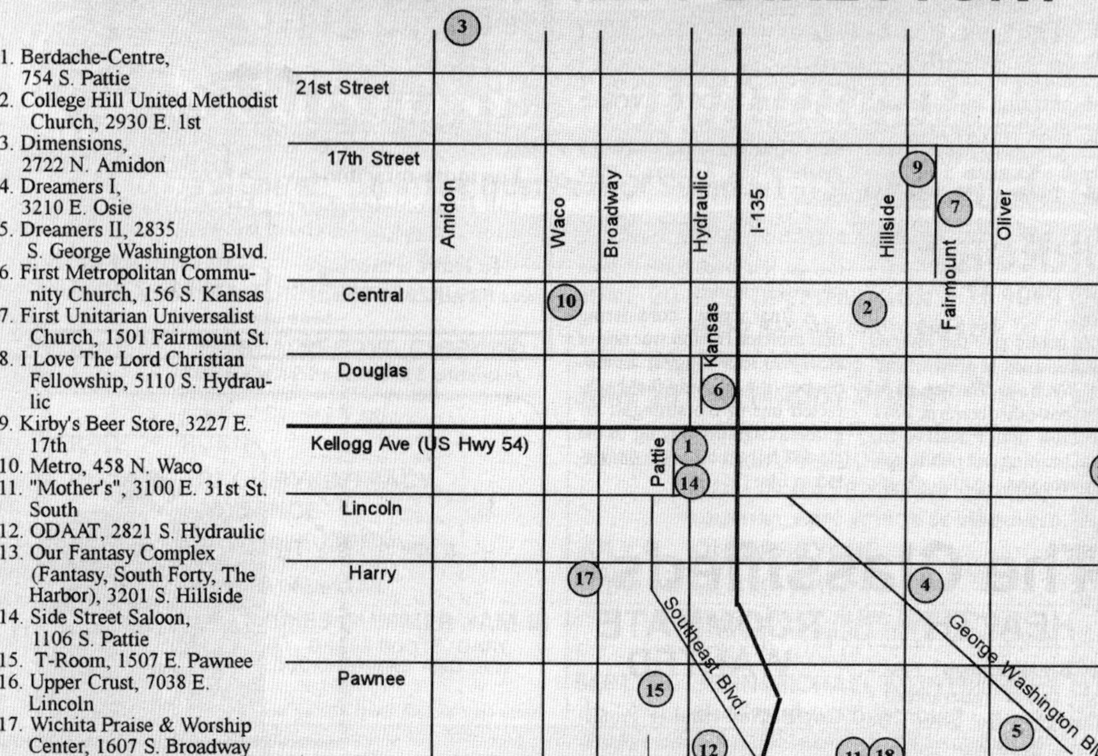

Page 52 1997 Pride Guide The Liberty Pr

WICHITA COMMUNITY DIRECTORY

1. Berdache-Centre, 754 S. Pattie
2. College Hill United Methodist Church, 2930 E. 1st
3. Dimensions, 2722 N. Amidon
4. Dreamers I, 3210 E. Osie
5. Dreamers II, 2835 S. George Washington Blvd.
6. First Metropolitan Community Church, 156 S. Kansas
7. First Unitarian Universalist Church, 1501 Fairmount St.
8. I Love The Lord Christian Fellowship, 5110 S. Hydraulic
9. Kirby's Beer Store, 3227 E. 17th
10. Metro, 458 N. Waco
11. "Mother's", 3100 E. 31st St. South
12. ODAAT, 2821 S. Hydraulic
13. Our Fantasy Complex (Fantasy, South Forty, The Harbor), 3201 S. Hillside
14. Side Street Saloon, 1106 S. Pattie
15. T-Room, 1507 E. Pawnee
16. Upper Crust, 7038 E. Lincoln
17. Wichita Praise & Worship Center, 1607 S. Broadway
18. Wichita Pride, Inc. HQ, 3102 E. 31st St. South

By the 1990s, a network of bars, religious organizations, and community venues had emerged across the city. The heart of the area was along Thirty-First Street, where Our Fantasy and the South Forty anchored an informal district that also included the R & R Brass Rail and a strip mall that housed Mother's Cards & Gifts, as well as the office for Wichita Pride and an LGBTQ coffee shop named the Kindred Kafe. (Courtesy of the *Liberty Press*.)

After several drag queens and their patrons received bad treatment at a local cafe, Linn Copeland opened a restaurant at the Our Fantasy Complex called the Harbor. The restaurant lasted through most of the 1990s; the site later became the location of Le Cafe and, even briefly, was an under-21 club called the Coop. (Courtesy of Tim Wood.)

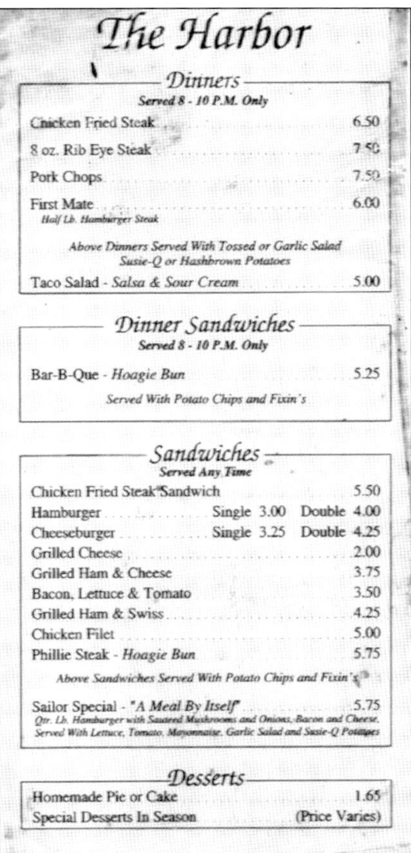

The Harbor

Dinners

Served 8 - 10 P.M. Only

Chicken Fried Steak	6.50
8 oz. Rib Eye Steak	7.50
Pork Chops	7.50
First Mate *Half Lb. Hamburger Steak*	6.00

Above Dinners Served With Tossed or Garlic Salad
Susie-Q or Hashbrown Potatoes

Taco Salad - *Salsa & Sour Cream*	5.00

Dinner Sandwiches

Served 8 - 10 P.M. Only

Bar-B-Que - *Hoagie Bun*	5.25

Served With Potato Chips and Fixin's

Sandwiches

Served Any Time

Chicken Fried Steak Sandwich		5.50
Hamburger	Single 3.00	Double 4.00
Cheeseburger	Single 3.25	Double 4.25
Grilled Cheese		2.00
Grilled Ham & Cheese		3.75
Bacon, Lettuce & Tomato		3.50
Grilled Ham & Swiss		4.25
Chicken Filet		5.00
Phillie Steak - *Hoagie Bun*		5.75

Above Sandwiches Served With Potato Chips and Fixin's

Sailor Special - *"A Meal By Itself"* *Qtr. Lb. Hamburger with Sauteed Mushrooms and Onions, Bacon and Cheese. Served With Lettuce, Tomato, Mayonnaise, Garlic Salad and Susie-Q Potatoes*	5.75

Desserts

Homemade Pie or Cake	1.65
Special Desserts In Season	(Price Varies)

Our Fantasy became a center for community events, including the Garden Party that took place right after the Kentucky Derby. Here, around the pool, revelers sport their fashion finery. (Courtesy of Virginia Norton.)

Late in the night of November 1, 1999, a fire broke out at the Our Fantasy Complex on south Hillside Street. Beginning in the site of Le Café in the old Harbor location, the blaze spread to most of the front part of the complex containing the Fantasy but left the South Forty intact. A few days later, the South Forty was back in operation with Big Mama Simone and Channing LaRue performing. It took several more months for the Fantasy part to rebuild. (Courtesy of Jennifer King.)

After a tour opening for Green Day, the nationally famous queer punks Pansy Division played Kirby's Beer Store to a packed house in 1994. Singer-songwriter Jon Ginoli recalled hearing about the tiny venue from Brit-punks the Mekons. The *Liberty Press* contributor Kim Card reported it was the "best show I saw all summer." Ginoli returned in 2009 for an acoustic performance and discussed his book *Deflowered: My Life in Pansy Division*. (Both images courtesy of the *Liberty Press*.)

Beginning in 1998, the community held a *Dining for Friends with Friends* event based on similar fundraisers in states like Virginia and Georgia. It was a series of simultaneously held dinner parties tied together with a common invitation and monetary donation. After individual dinners concluded, all participants gathered at a single location for dessert. Here is one such event where Fritz Capone is in full glory at the Scottish Rite Temple auditorium. (Courtesy of Jennifer King.)

Four

To the Stars through Difficulties

You have to march in your own town. I realized that if I marched in New York City, but I was afraid to march here, that's just another closet.

—Martin Mendoza

Kansas had become one of the nation's test beds for conservative resurgence on a range of social issues. The Kansas sodomy law, for example, remained in place in spite of efforts to repeal it, only to be ruled unconstitutional in the US Supreme Court's 2003 ruling on *Lawrence v. Texas*. Marriage and partnership remained another issue. A 2005 US census report showed a 68 percent increase in same-sex households, although Kansans solidified an opposition to same-sex marriage in the state constitution. Laws and policies that targeted LGBTQ persons, such as the Defense of Marriage campaigns, however, galvanized LGBTQ political and advocacy efforts such as Equality Kansas. The Supreme Court case of *Obergefell v. Hodges*, meanwhile, allowed a new era for couples to legally marry. Events such as Art Aid connected the community with allies across the city. Growing acceptance in many areas, coupled with the emergence of social media, helped people become more integrated into everyday life.

The 2000s brought a time of transition. The community lost icons such as Big Mama Simone, Fritz Capone, Linn Copeland, Kristi Parker, and Stephanie Mott. Their passing coincided with the end of the *Liberty Press* and the closing of clubs such as Our Fantasy. It was a time of transition as older generations looked back on the changes that had taken place. Meanwhile, new generations emerged. Issues of gender identity and the trans community reshaped a conversation that has continued into the future.

Founded in the fall of 2002, the Heart of America Men's Chorus functioned under the direction of Howard Webb during its first years. It became known for its performances, from HIV/AIDS benefits to annual Christmas shows. (Above, courtesy of Heart of America Men's Chorus; left, courtesy of Benjamin and Curtis Breese-Isley.)

Although well known within the LGBTQ community, with many LGBTQ members, the chorus did not identify itself as a gay organization. In recent years, however, under the direction of director Deeann Zogelman, the organization has now become much more openly an LGBTQ group. (Both images courtesy of Benjamin Breese-Isley.)

The Wichita Bears were both a social and fundraising group. Social activities included Bears in Heat, while events like La Cage Aux Bears raised money for LGBTQ and other causes. Among the more popular fundraisers was a cookbook, seen below. (Both images courtesy of Benjamin and Curtis Breese-Isley.)

Cookbook

Bears in the Heat VII

Wichita Bears Wichita, Kansas July 10-12, 2009

At one Aux Cage Aux Bears event, Ben Breese-Isley (left) with Scott Hollander (also known as Mama Hirst) and Francis Foster are pictured. (Courtesy of Benjamin and Curtis Breese-Isley.)

The leather community in Wichita traces back to the 1970s. The latest of which was the Wichita Organization of Leather Fetishists (WOOLF), which began in 2002 and lasted until 2018. Its mission was to provide education, promote goodwill, and build inter-community relationships. They promoted safe, sane, and consensual play, and they became known for their annual Chili Feed at J's Lounge and "Arrest-Your-Friends" at South Forty Bar. (Courtesy of Jim Martinson.)

Master C has been in the leather lifestyle since the 1980s, honored by his Wichita leather tribe as a master in 2008. He served as the president of the Wichita Organization of Leather Fetishists (WOOLF) for several years, producing WOOLF Leather Camp, Great Plains Leather Sir contest, and the Central Plains Drummer North America contest. He taught various leather/BDSM classes across the United States and wrote a regular column for the *Liberty Press*. He is in a long-term triad relationship with two leather boys, boy John and boy Mike. (Courtesy of the *Liberty Press*.)

Among the oldest leather organizations in the city was the Wichita Linemen, a somewhat joking reference that conveniently was also a common local men's blue-collar job and the title of a Glen Campbell song celebrating them. It lasted only a short time, but several of the same individuals formed the Pegasus Motorcycle Club, a group that eventually became the Pegasus Men's Club, which lasted into the early 1990s. (Above, courtesy of Jennifer King; right, courtesy of Jim Martinson.)

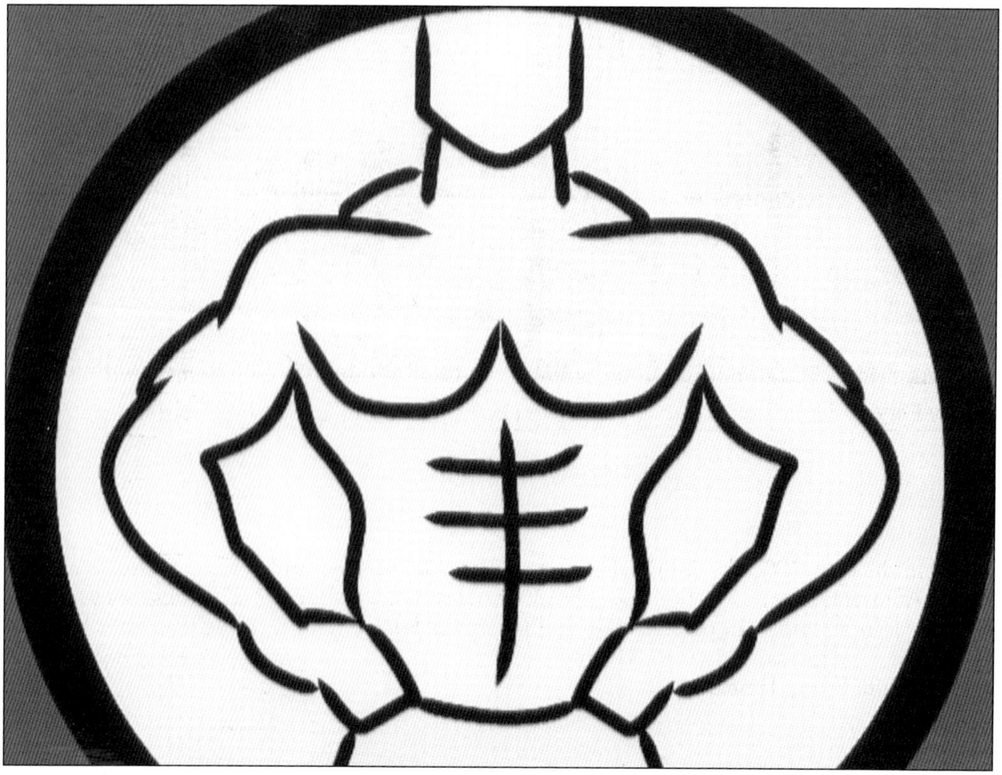

As part of Positive Direction's direct advocacy, a street outreach program was developed in 2011, which eventually became the host of weekly Bitchy Bingo events at venues that included Rain Cafe and Bar. By 2014, it was hosting events at its own location, which is now B&B Bingo Hall at 41st Street South and Seneca Street, and other local organizations had also participated, including the Center of Wichita, Wichita Pride, and GLSEN. (Courtesy of Positive Directions.)

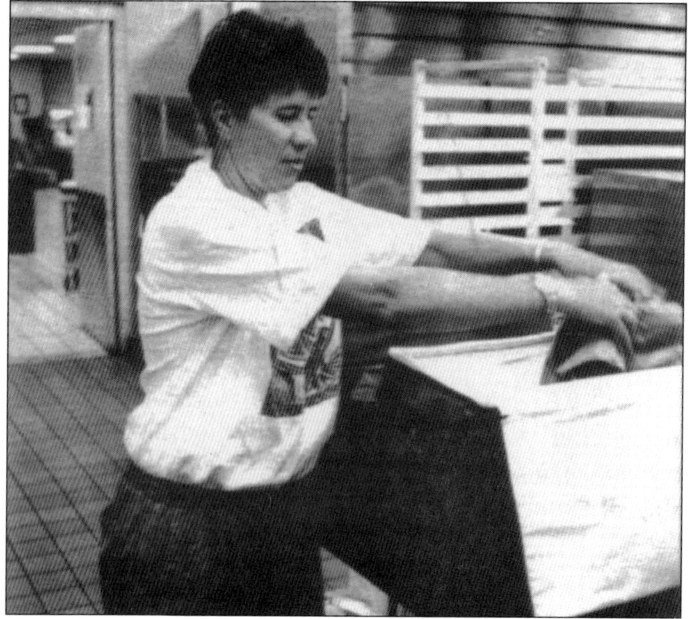

In 1997, the Care Coordination Team started a food delivery program for those living with HIV in Wichita. Nonprofit *Meals on Wheels* had previously provided the service, but by 1996, its funding declined, and it discontinued HIV services. The Daily Bread Program was proposed at CCT and a corresponding food pantry housed at the ConnectCare offices was established. By 1999, it had 22 clients receiving a minimum of twice-weekly meals. (Courtesy of Positive Directions.)

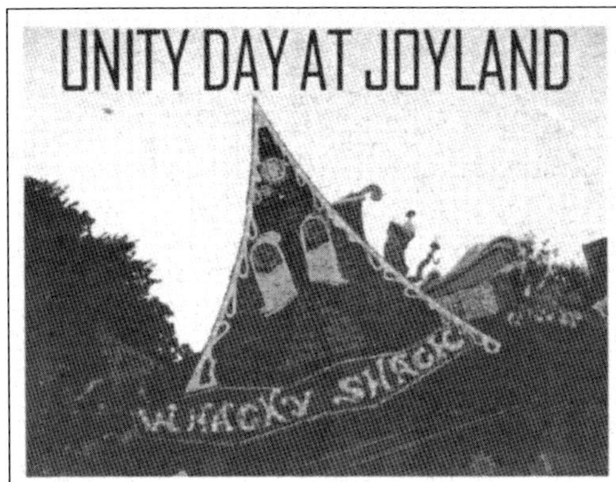

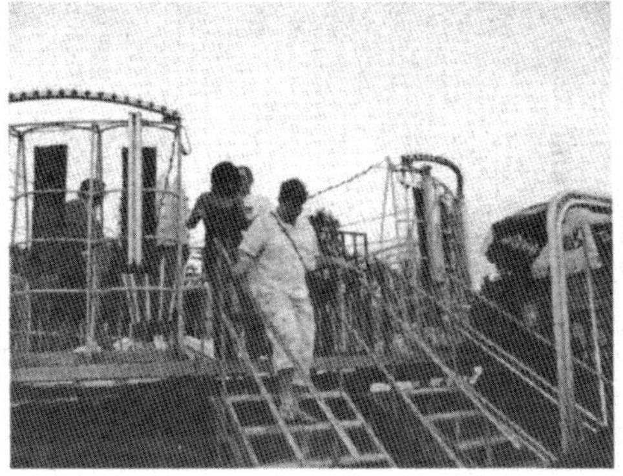

UNITY DAY AT JOYLAND
WHACKY SHACK
Unity Day 2004, a fundraiser for Positive Directions and friends, was held June 16th.

Hosted in the early 2000s by Positive Directions, That Gay Group!, and Wichita Prime Timers at Joyland Amusement Park. In 2004, roughly 600 people attended, Don "Kyle" Jacobs, below. Adult beverages were provided to those of age, and musical entertainment included DJs, the Heart of America Men's Chorus, and Fritz and Follies. (Above, courtesy of the *Liberty Press*; below, courtesy of the Wichita Prime Timers.)

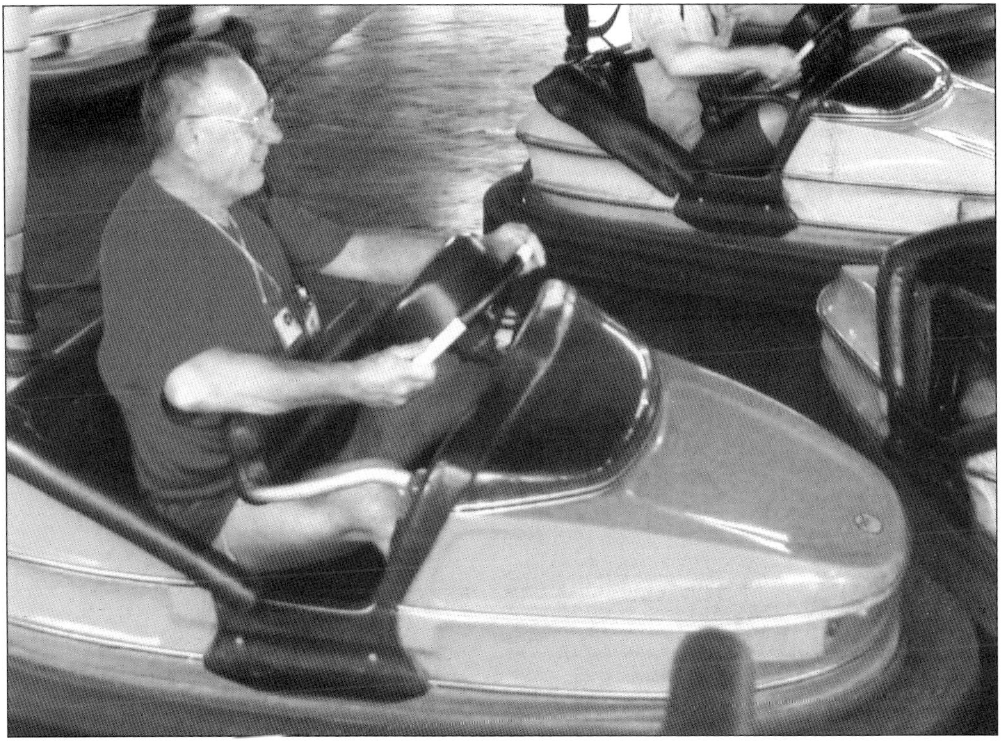

By the 2000s, a number of religious denominations had congregations and were affirming LGBTQ persons and groups to advocate for broader official recognition. Other traditions saw outspoken ministers. Some traditions, like the Unitarians and Unity, had long traditions of activism on progressive causes and had come to embrace LGBTQ persons as one of those causes. This allowed churches like Pine Valley Christian to become important voices of support. (Courtesy of Pine Valley Christian Church.)

Denominations like the Episcopal Church, on the other hand, had to function within regional and national networks, resulting in groups like Integrity to push for same-sex blessings and other support. In Wichita, the local Integrity chapter was formed in 2000. It operated at a time when the Episcopal Church was wrestling with the ordination of openly gay Bishop Gene Robinson in the face of resistance on the part of conservative Anglicans. Here, Integrity members participate in the Dining with Friends for Friends HIV/AIDS event at St. James Episcopal Church. (Courtesy of Jennifer King.)

GOD LOVES ALL OF US

VOTE NO TO HATE

In 1996, Kansas passed a law that banned same-sex marriage and denied the recognition of same-sex marriages performed in other states. In the spring of 2005, same-sex marriage had become a cause for the state's growing social conservative movement, with fears that earlier legal restrictions could be weekend or overruled. In response, conservatives had put to the voters a constitutional amendment banning same-sex marriage. Kansans voted in favor of the amendment by 2-1 on April 5, 2005. (Both images courtesy of KU.)

Diane Silver remembered that "as awful as it is, the marriage ban pushed us into creating the Kansas Equality Coalition." In June 2004, figures including Patrick Hutchinson and Tom Witt, seen here at a rally in Topeka being told by capital police his flag poles constituted weapons, had incorporated the group Equality Kansas as a key lobbying body to advocate for LGBTQ concerns at the state legislature. The first Kansas Equality Day took place in Topeka on February 22, 2007. (Both images courtesy of Kerry Wilks.)

Reading a letter by Al Gore in *Out* magazine inspired 19-year-old Jason Dilts to step forward to help with the campaign. This led to being an active voice in local Democratic activities and in 2002, he became executive director of the Sedgwick County Democratic Party. For the next seven years, he worked to recruit candidates and support during the 2000s' key sociopolitical battles in Kansas. (Courtesy of Jason Dilts.)

Activism continued on local levels, with protests like this one in Old Town in favor of gay marriage and efforts to shape things in the state legislature. (Courtesy of James and Curtis Breese-Isley.)

In October 2014, the Tenth Circuit Court ruled in favor of marriage equality. Kerry Wilks, chair of the South Central Chapter of Equality Kansas, and Donna DiTrani went to the Sedgwick County Courthouse to file for a marriage license and were denied. They became ACLU plaintiffs suing Kansas, with another couple, for the right to get married. This photograph shows DiTrani and Wilks, with chief counsel for the ACLU of Kansas Doug Bonney. The Kansas federal judge upheld their case, and the US Supreme Court upheld that decision. Following the lifting of the injunction, clergy gathered on the steps of the Wichita historic courthouse to perform a "Make it Legal" ceremony, below. DiTrani and Wilks were eventually allowed to (legally) marry after the *Obergefell v. Hodges* decision in June 2015. (Above, courtesy of Kerry Wilks; below, courtesy of Pine Valley Christian Church.)

A couple since the 1980s, Colleen "Coke" Didier and Jennifer King were well known in the community. Finally, with *Obergefell v. Hodges*, they were able to marry legally with Mother Dawn Frankfurt of St. James Episcopal presiding. (Courtesy of Jennifer King.)

In many cases, partners married for ceremonial reasons but with no legal standing. With the Supreme Court decision couples like Ben and Curtis Breese-Isley held second ceremonies now with official recognition. Other couples had waited until same-sex marriage was indeed legal before tying the knot. (Courtesy of Benjamin and Curtis Breese-Isley.)

In the 1990s, Kristi Parker (right) and Sharon "Vinnie" Levin (left) formed Wichita Pride, Inc. and ran it until 2001. In the early 2000s, Wichita Pride as an official organization had ceased to function although informal events continued. In 2006, a new Wichita Pride was incorporated with renewed citywide Pride taking place in 2007. (Courtesy of Deb Davis and Staci Steddum.)

Women Without Purses was formed in 1992 as a queer all-women group led by Carla Venable. The band often performed at notable bars, such as Kirby's, and became a more prominent piece of the Wichita LGBTQ community. In total, they produced three original studio albums during their peak in the 1990s and early 2000s. They remain active with shows occurring in the last five years. (Courtesy of Women Without Purses.)

Wichita's first celebration of National Coming Out Day, held yearly on October 11, was hosted by Brent Kennedy at the old Naftzger Park gazebo in 2010. Speakers included local community organizer Sally Morse, Rev. Jackie Carter, and at the time, Kansas House candidate Dan Manning. GLSEN Kansas took over hosting in 2015. (Courtesy of Brent Kennedy.)

Trans Day of Remembrance is a national event held on November 20th starting in 1999. One of the first hosted in Wichita was on Wichita State's campus by That Gay Group! in 2009. A display case was filled with white flowers and the names of those lost. The next year they held a reading of names in the Campus Activity Center Theater. Spectrum: LGBTQ & Allies has continued hosting the event ever since. (Courtesy of WSU Spectrum group.)

A major shift in public attitudes included the rise of popular programs such as *Will & Grace*, *Ellen*, and *Queer as Folk*, which was a North American adaptation of a British series that came out in 2000. The series could also be a social event, as when Dudley Toevs, seen here, held gatherings of 10–12 men to watch the series and follow the characters' lives. (Courtesy of Dudley Toevs.)

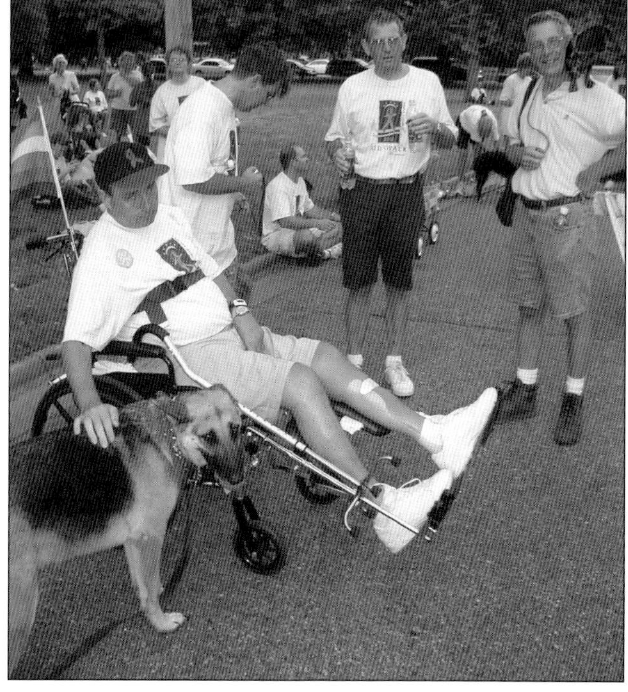

Beginning in 1993 the AIDS Walk-Run was one of the first events hosted by the Care Coordination Team. By 1999, it had moved to Riverside Park and was raising over $15,000 annually for people living with HIV/AIDS. As of 2019, the walk was so successful, it grew into an all-day event including a market and music festival. (Courtesy of Positive Directions and the Wichita Prime Timers.)

A graduate of West Point, Dan Manning served in the US Military in Korea. After returning to Wichita, he turned his attention to activism efforts, including an unsuccessful bid for the Kansas House of Representatives in the 91st District. Manning (right) appears here as the co-grand marshal of the 2011 Pride Fest along with his fellow soldier Dan Choi (left) who himself became famous for chaining himself to the White House Fence in uniform in 2010 to protest "Don't Ask, Don't Tell." (Courtesy of Dave Quick.)

Older gay men, who had led the first struggles in the 1970s found it harder to connect with a community focused on youth. In 1998, Dale Sneeringer and Jim Funk helped organize the Wichita Prime Timers as a social and community group. It is part of a global network of Prime Timer organizations. (Courtesy of Derek Landwehr.)

In 2008, the newly ordained Rev. Jackie Carter became the pastor of First Metropolitan Community Church of Kansas. With a tireless focus on social justice, one of her more famous actions was performing 15 simultaneous same-sex marriage ceremonies on the steps of the Sedgwick County Court House in 2014. (Courtesy of Dave Quick and Jackie Carter.)

When it was formed, First Metropolitan Community Church was a refuge where LGBTQ persons could worship without hiding who they were. It had served as a hub of activism during the AIDS crisis and was a place where countless organizations met. By the 2000s, LGBTQ persons had a range of options for worship while other issues, such as poverty emerged as pressing issues. In response, the congregation renamed itself Table of Hope and has become best known for its food pantry and other social services. (Courtesy of Table of Hope Metropolitan Community Church.)

Friends of Linn Copeland gather at the Our Fantasy Complex pond to spread her ashes after her death from lung cancer in 2005. Our Fantasy's duck pond was one of Linn's favorite places and remains her final resting place, including a commemorative plaque. Big Mama Simone died at the same time, and his memorial took place at the same time. Jennifer King recalled that it was one of the increasingly rare times the community as a whole came together. (Both images courtesy of Jennifer King.)

Born in Coffeyville, Bruce A. McKinney attended Wichita State University from 1971 to 1975. His activism started with the WSU Homophiles in 1976 and continued well into the 2000s with the Pride Committee, Kansas Equality Coalition, and the Center of Wichita, among others. An important collector of LGBTQ history, his materials were donated to the University of Kansas in 2009. McKinney passed away in February 2020. (Courtesy of Dave Quick and Jennifer King.)

Topeka-based Stephanie Mott was a leader in the state's transgender community, serving as the founder of the Transgender Faith Tour and the president/executive director of the Kansas Statewide Transgender Education Project (K-STEP), as well as active work with groups such as Equality Kansas. Her statewide work inspired and supported activism in Wichita, and following her passing in 2019, Wichita State University renamed its Harvey Milk Award to the Stephanie Mott Living Authentically Award. (Courtesy of Dave Quick.)

Kristi Parker was an influential figure in the Wichita, and later Kansas, LGBTQ scene. Parker, a Wichita native and Wichita State University alum, worked as the premier LGBTQ+ journalist from 1994 to 2018 in Wichita. She published the award-winning journal the *Liberty Press* in the early 1990s as a way to share information regarding ongoing queer events in the city. She grew quickly in publication and reputation, soon releasing copies of the paper in various other cities across Kansas. (Courtesy of Wichita State University Belonging Plaza.)

THE GAYLY Regional

AUGUST 2024 Vol. 43 Issue 4 www.GAYLY.com FREE

The District Hotel becoming an all-inclusive resort

Full story on pages 22 & 23

When the *Liberty Press* ceased publication, the *Gayly*, which began as the *Gayly Oklahoman* in 1983, became the region's main LGBTQ paper. (Courtesy of Robin Dormer.)

"We thought it would be fun," recalled Dave Barker, seen here, when he and Randy Whisnant opened The OtherSide in a building adjacent to J's Lounge. A few years later, the club moved to the southwest corner of Cleveland Street and Central Avenue. Among its events was a women's event called GLOW for "Gotta Love OtherSide Women." (Courtesy of David Barker)

More than bar owners, LGBTQ persons have been attorneys, doctors, restaurateurs, florists, and other entrepreneurs. Sometimes, they needed to be circumspect about their orientation out of fear of losing clientele and customers. In more recent years, organizations such as Proud of Wichita, an LGBTQ business association, have represented a business community that is more open. (Courtesy Proud of Wichita.)

In 2010, a member of the board of Wichita Pride revived the concept of a community center under the name "the Center of Human Rights." With the help of community leaders like Tom Witt, Sally Morse, and Kristi Parker, the organization quickly flourished. Renamed to the Center of Wichita, it currently hosts various support groups, a resource library, and an archive; sponsors the LGBT Health Coalition; and helps other organizations like Camp Sunflower. (Courtesy of the Center of Wichita.)

In 2012, the Kansas Legislature passed a law saying that librarians could be held personally and legally liable for any materials that local authorities deemed offensive. Soon after, librarians across the state felt pressured to divest their collections of LGBTQ materials and reached out to the center. What began as a collection of 100 books from some locals and a few librarians near Hays, Kansas, has now grown to a collection of almost 2,000 volumes spanning back to the 1930s. (Courtesy of the Center of Wichita.)

Our Fantasy closed in 2015. Soon after developer Rob Snyder purchased the Our Fantasy site while former Travis Bryson and DJ Michael Kasselman, seen here, leased and reopened the South Forty as Fantasy South 40 as an entrepreneur, while the Fantasy side continued to operate as a separate venture. (Courtesy of Our Fantasy.)

The venue at 3210 East Osie Street was Ralph's in the 1990s. By the 2000s, the site housed a number of bars that tended to cater to the lesbian community including the Corner and particularly, the Store, where Virginia Norton, seated in this image, is celebrating her birthday. (Courtesy of Virginia Norton.)

The Wichita State LGBTQ organization remained as Ten Percent from 1993 until being renamed That Gay Group! in 2000. It gained its current name, Spectrum: LGBTQ & Allies, in 2014. Since 2011, the students have hosted an annual campus drag show and now have a Lavender Graduation where LGBTQ students are honored with a purple chord. (Courtesy of WSU Spectrum group.)

WE ALL SHARE WICHITA'S PARKS

Some activities should be shared in the privacy of your own homes

For your safety, and so everyone can enjoy our parks, please take intimate activities indoors.

For decades, the community associated the police with raids, arrests, and harassment. Things began to change when Gordon Ramsay became police chief in 2016. With a focus on education and community relations instead of just enforcement, the department tasked two officers, Sgt. Don Kimble and Sgt. Vanessa Rusco, as liaisons regularly work with the community. Among their efforts was working with the Center in a campaign to discourage illicit behavior in public parks. In 2016, the Wichita Police force had a presence at the Pride parade for the first time, and now LGBTQ members are part of the Cultural Diversity Awareness Panel to train officers at the police academy.

After the 2010s, Wichita State took a more active role in supporting its LGBTQ students. This was through the efforts of sociology professor Dr. Jenny Pearson (pictured above left) and the Office of Diversity and Inclusion (previously the Office of Multicultural Affairs), and later, LGBTQ coordinator Brad Thomison (above right). Thomison was also the owner of Club Boomerang, where he performed as Divinity Masters (below). Thomison recalled that the persona of Divinity Masters emerged in a thrift store on New Year's Eve 2007 when "a pink and black prom dress just screamed 'drag queen!'" (Both images courtesy of WSU and the *Sunflower*.)

Camp Sunflower started in 2018 in partnership with several local organizations including Pine Valley Christian, GLSEN, and the Center of Wichita. The nonprofit provides a yearly week-long camp experience for LGBTQ youth in a safe and supportive environment, even offering sponsorship for hardship attendees who otherwise would not be able to afford to go. (Courtesy of GLSEN.)

Originally the Gay Lesbian and Straight Education Network, GLSEN is a national anti-bullying organization for LGBTQ students that publishes the yearly school climate survey. The Kansas chapter was started in 2014 by Liz Hamor to help support queer youth by providing advocacy and outreach in education facilities, and by hosting annual events including Day of Silence and Trans Day of Visibility. (Courtesy of Brent Kennedy.)

ORG. No.: 10010100

First Published in the Wichita Eagle on October 29, 2021

ORDINANCE NO. 51-654

AN ORDINANCE CREATING CHAPTER 2.06 OF THE CODE OF THE CITY OF WICHITA PERTAINING TO NONDISCRIMINATION.

BE IT ORDAINED BY THE GOVERNING BODY OF THE CITY OF WICHITA, KANSAS:

SECTION 1. Section 2.06.010 of the Code of the City of Wichita, is hereby created to read as follows:

"**Policy Prohibiting Discrimination.**
The practice or policy of discrimination against persons by reason of their age, color, disability, familial status, gender identity, genetic information, national origin or ancestry, race, religion, sex, sexual orientation, veteran status or any other factor protected by law ("protected class") is a matter of concern to the City, since such discrimination not only threatens the rights and privileges of the inhabitants of the City but also menaces the institutions and foundations of a free democratic state. It is hereby declared the policy of the City, in exercise of its police power for the protection of the public safety, health and general welfare, for the maintenance of business and good government, and for the promotion of the City's trade and commerce, to eliminate and prevent discrimination or segregation based on a protected class. It is further declared to be the policy of the City to assure equal opportunity and encouragement for every person, regardless of their membership in a protected class, to secure and hold, without discrimination, employment in any field of work or labor for which the person is otherwise properly qualified; to assure equal opportunity for all persons within this City to full and equal public accommodations and the full and equal use and enjoyment of the services, facilities, privileges and advantages of all governmental departments or agencies, and to assure equal opportunity for all persons within this City in housing, without distinction on account of membership in a protected class."

SECTION 2. Section 2.06.020 of the Code of the City of Wichita, is hereby created to read as follows:

"**Nondiscrimination in Contracting.**
(a) It is the policy of the City to promote the principles of equal opportunity in its contracting activities by assuring that those seeking to do business with the City will treat contractors, subcontractors, and employees equally and will not engage in discrimination against their contractors, subcontractors, or employees because of their age, color, disability, familial status, gender identity, genetic information, national origin or ancestry, race, religion, sex, sexual orientation, veteran status or any other factor protected by law ("protected class").

(b) It is also the policy of the City to ensure that work performed on behalf of the City is done in a cost effective and high-quality manner. Employees who are treated fairly are more productive in their jobs and less likely to change jobs, thus helping to ensure that government contracts are both cost effective and completed in a professional manner.

(c) All City contracts for goods or services shall include provisions prohibiting discrimination

Sexual Orientation means an individual's actual or perceived (by the individual or another) emotional, romantic or sexual attraction to other people, such as heterosexual, homosexual, bisexual, pansexual or asexual.

Unlawful Discriminatory Practices means those practices prohibited by Section 2.06.050 of this Chapter."

SECTION 4. Section 2.06.040 of the Code of the City of Wichita, is hereby created to read as follows:

"**Civil Rights Declared.**
(a) The right of an otherwise qualified person to be free from discrimination because of that person's age, color, disability, familial status, gender identity, genetic information, national origin or ancestry, race, religion, sex, sexual orientation or military or veteran status is recognized as, and declared to be, a civil right. This right shall include, but not be limited to, all of the following:

(1) The right to obtain and hold employment and the benefits associated therewith without discrimination.

(2) The right to the full enjoyment of any of the accommodations, advantages, facilities or privileges of any place of public accommodation without discrimination.

(3) The right to engage in property transactions, including obtaining housing for rental or sale and credit therefor, without discrimination.

(4) The right to exercise any right granted under this Chapter without suffering coercion or retaliation."

SECTION 5. Section 2.06.050 of the Code of the City of Wichita, is hereby created to read as follows:

"**Unlawful Discriminatory Practices.**
In order to protect specific individuals within the City from discrimination on the basis of their membership in a legally-protected class, it shall be a duty of each individual or entity doing business within the City to not commit the following Unlawful Discriminatory Practices:

(a) Employment — It shall be an Unlawful Discriminatory Practice for an Employer to refuse to hire or employ, or to discharge from employment or to otherwise discriminate against an

SECTION 7. Section 2.06.070 of the Code of the City of Wichita, is hereby created to read as follows:

"**Enforcement.**
(a) An Aggrieved Individual may file a written complaint with the City Clerk that the individual has been, or is being, subjected to an alleged Unlawful Discriminatory Practice(s) as prohibited by this Chapter. The complaint may be filed personally or through an attorney (or if a minor, through the minor's parent, legal guardian or attorney) and shall be completed on a form provided by the City. The complaint form shall state the names and contact information of the Aggrieved Individual, the individual(s) and/or entity/entities alleged to have committed the Unlawful Discriminatory Practice(s), a description of the alleged unlawful conduct, and all other information as may be required by the form provided by the City. The complaint form shall only be considered complete if all information required by the City's form has been provided to the extent such information is reasonably available to the Aggrieved Individual.

(b) The complaint form must be filed within one-hundred eighty (180) Days of the alleged Unlawful Discriminatory Practice, unless the act complained of constitutes a continuing pattern or practice of discrimination, in which event, it must be filed within one-hundred eighty (180) Days of the last act of discrimination.

(c) The complaint may be referred to a mediator selected by the City Manager from a list of mediators approved in advance by the City Council. Mediation costs will be paid by the City.

(d) If mediation is not successfully completed within sixty (60) Days of the referral, or a party chooses not to pursue mediation, the complaint shall be referred to the Investigator.

(e) Upon receipt of a completed complaint, the Investigator shall notify the Respondent(s) of the complaint, providing sufficient details related to the complaint so the Respondent(s) may respond. The Investigator shall give the Respondent(s) thirty (30) Days to file a written answer to the complaint, and to provide any documentation or evidence related to the complaint. The Investigator may, at the request of Respondent(s), extend the answer period an additional thirty (30) Days. If the Respondent accused of violating the provisions of this Chapter is the City, the City will engage an independent Investigator who shall not otherwise be an Employee, agent, or contractor of the City. If the Respondent is the City, nothing in this ordinance shall affect the employee grievance processes in contract or policy.

(f) Following the conclusion of the answer period, the Investigator may initiate an investigation period, requesting that the Aggrieved Individual and/or Respondent(s)

Mayor Brandon Whipple proposed the new nondiscrimination ordinance in June 2021, receiving continuous backlash until the vote in late September. Wichita's 2021 annual fall Pride parade occurred days before the vote and campaigned for the passing of the ordinance. It passed on October 12, 2021. (Courtesy of Brandon Whipple.)

Born in Wichita and raised in Houston, Rick Muma's background in public health shaped his career as a faculty member at Wichita State University in the College of Health Professions. In 2021, he became the 15th president of Wichita State University. His husband of 15 years, Rick Case of Wakefield, Kansas, became the university's first "first husband." (Courtesy of Wichita State University.)

The Sisters of Perpetual Indulgence are an international organization founded on Easter Sunday 1979 in San Francisco. Local branches include the City of Fountains Sisters in Kansas City and Emerald City Sisters in Wichita. Described as "21st-century nuns with a calling," Emerald City members wear winged coronets as homage to the Air Capital of the World. They support Universal Joy with the tenets "Power through joy, advocacy through love."

Started in 2022 by James Boyd and his partner at Leaf and Stone Apothecary, the Big Gay Market was originally a small street fair of 30 vendors and artists around R Coffee House in Riverside. By 2024, it boasted over 130 booths and took over most of Riverside Park.

In 2024, the Wichita Jewish community launched its first Pride seder. Usually associated with Passover, a seder is a commemorative meal and can mark other important events. Here, the foods use the colors of the rainbow flag, along with a rainbow-tinted challah.

A team of participants shows a flag that merges the LGBTQ rainbow flag colors with the Wichita city flag and includes a Native American sun symbol that represents "home."

When the public thinks of photographs of LGBTQ life, typically they think of images like this one, showing activism, rainbow flags, perhaps events at clubs or drag shows. In reality, LGBTQ life is quiet and ordinary and looks like everyday life in the rest of society. The image below, of a gathering at Bo's Bash, is perhaps a more accurate depiction of what LGBTQ Wichita has been like. (Above, courtesy of Jackie Carter; below, courtesy of Jennifer King.)

BIBLIOGRAPHY

Baker, Gilbert. *Rainbow Warrior: My Life in Color.* Chicago: the Gilbert Baker Estate, 2019.

Barr, James. *Quatrefoil: A Modern Novel.* Boston: Alyson Publications, Inc. 1950.

Bruce McKinney Collection at the Spencer Library, University of Kansas

Fejez, Fred. *Gay Rights and the Moral Panic: The Origins of America's Debate on Homosexuality*. New York: Palgrave Macmillan, 2010.

Humphreys, Laud. *Tearoom Trade: Impersonal Sex in Public Places (Observations)*, 2nd Ed. New York: Routledge, 1975.

Janovy, C.J. *No Place Like Home: Lessons in Activism from LBGT Kansas.* Lawrence, KS: University Press of Kansas, 2018.

Marquez, Hugo. "Understanding Homosexuality in Postwar Kansas," *Fairmount Folio* (2010): 1–26.

Rose-Mocky, Katherine. *Liberating Lawrence: Gay Activism in the 1970s at the University of Kansas.* Lawrence, KS: University Press of Kansas, 2024.

The *Liberty Press*, available at the Center of Wichita.

Thornton, Tyler, "Wichita's Gay Rights Ordinance No. 35-242: Opposition and Activism *Fairmount Folio* (2012): 140–64.

www.gayly.com

Consistent with our mission to preserve history on a local level, this book was printed in South Carolina on American-made paper and manufactured entirely in the United States. Products carrying the accredited Forest Stewardship Council (FSC) label are printed on 100 percent FSC-certified paper.